theTimberline Review

SUMMER / FALL 2016

NO. 3

A publication of Willamette Writers

the Timberline Review

PUBLISHER	Peter R Field
EDITOR	Pam Wells
POETRY EDITORS	Sue Fagalde Lick, John Clark Vincent
FOUNDING EDITORS	Peter R Field & Pam Wells
READERS	Joan Macbeth, Randal Houle, Eddie Lueken, Maren Anderson
WEB & MEDIA SUPPORT	Kate Ristau
DESIGN & LAYOUT	Pam Wells

TIMBERLINE REVIEW ADVISORY BOARD
Brian Doyle, Per Henningsgaard

The Timberline Review is published twice a year by Willamette Writers, Inc., a 501(c)(3) nonprofit organization founded in 1965. Editorial offices: 2108 Buck Street, West Linn, OR 97068

Print subscription: $22/year (2 issues) or $40/2 years (4 issues) plus shipping. Please visit timberlinereview.com to subscribe and to purchase additional copies and back issues.

Submissions generally will be accepted during two reading periods:
January 1 - April 15 for the Summer/Fall issue and July 1 - October 15 for the Winter/Spring issue. Electronic submissions only, please. See timberlinereview.com for guidelines.

ISBN 978-0-9964618-2-5

Typeset in Caslon Pro and Lithos Pro
Printed in Centralia, Washington

COMMUNITY OF LITERARY MAGAZINES & PRESSES
W W W . C L M P . O R G

ON THE COVER: "Susan" by Judy Biesanz
Judy Biesanz is a painter who lives and works in Portland. She attended the New York Studio School and received her BA in painting from the Pacific Northwest College of Art in 2000. More of her work can be seen at judybiesanz.com.

Black & white cover photo by David Wells

CONTENTS

6   Editor's Notes

7   From the Publisher's Desk

NONFICTION & ESSAY

Variations on a Beginning | M. ALLEN CUNNINGHAM
A personal essay in fifteen parts

9   Variation [1]

9   Variation [2]

10   Variation [3]

25   Variation [4]

32   **In My Defense** | BRIAN DOYLE

35   Variation [5]

46   Variation [6]

61   Variation [7]

80   Variation [8]

81   **Why I Didn't Go to the Firehouse** | SOPHFRONIA SCOTT

97   Variation [9]

99   **My Monastic Dwelling at Hood Canal** | MARC HUDSON

109   Variation [10]

121   Variation [11]

129   Variation [12]

142   Variation [13]

143   **Echo Moth** | ROBERT VIVIAN

145   Variation [14]

157   Variation [15]

FICTION

14 A Bath in the Ganges | ROBERT HAMBURGER

62 Foot in America | DAVID SCHULTZ

130 No Telling | JODY LISBERGER

146 Praying In Souzhou | ROSANNA STAFFA

POETRY

11 Two Bottles | CHRIS ABBATE

13 The Door in the River | PEPPER TRAIL

26 The Eel Catcher | ANN E. MICHAEL

27 On a Deschutes County Road in Winter | DAVID MELVILLE

28 We Were Always the Good | CLARA MAE BARNHART

30 Lost Boy: Peter Pan's Mother Has Her Say | BRITTNEY CORRIGAN

37 Nomenclature | ANDREA HOLLANDER

39 The Apricot Tree | RICHARD SPILMAN
   Moving in
   Interpreting Dreams
   What Love Leaves Behind
   The Names of Things
   Apricot Tree

43 Lessons in Picking Fruit | PETER SERCHUK

44 After the Blizzard | EMILY RANSDELL

48 Just South of the Bixby Canyon Bridge | TRAVIS TRUAX

50 To My Parents on their Separation | CHRIS ABBATE

52 The Turnover | PAULANN PETERSEN

54 Joe's Daughter | PETER SERCHUK

56 Doubt | ANDREA HOLLANDER

57 Inheritance | CATHERINE ARRA

92 Pantoum for the End of the World | PEPPER TRAIL

94 Bud Light in an Idaho diner during another shooting
   | DYLAN D. DEBELIS

95 Pincushion | LESLIE MILLS

96 Found, October 18, 1848 | FREDERICK W. BASSETT

110 Damn it, we're all so lonely | PENELOPE SCAMBLY SCHOTT

112 Portable Typewriter on a Small Leaky Boat | ANNIE LIGHTHART

113 Echolalia | C. WADE BENTLEY

114 To the barista at Starbucks who told me Carmel Macchiato isn't the heroine in *Two Gentlemen of Verona* | DOUG STONE

116 Old | C. WADE BENTLEY

117 Reflections at the Checkout | LOUISE BARDEN

119 Gifts | ELIZABETH KUELBS

120 For Portland teenagers drinking under bridges | DYLAN D. DEBELIS

122 Sure-Footed | MILTON BATES

123 Whose blood is this | DANIEL ARISTI

124 Leave | HEATHER WHITED

126 Two Kinds of Silence | HEATHER WHITED

139 In Good Voice | SARAH BOKICH

140 Oppressive Bounty | LESLIE MILLS

141 The Word Alabaster | GEORGE DREW

154 Revival | CHRISTY STEVENS

156 Leaving Sicily | CATHERINE ARRA

158 Contributors

164 Acknowledgments

167 About Willamette Writers

Editor's Notes

MORE OFTEN THAN NOT, when I sit down to write something, I'm haunted with the question of how to begin. Even now, introducing our third issue, I keep trying out different ways to get started. Type, delete, type, delete, change fonts—that's got to help. Palatino? Avenir? No, I'm in a Caslon state of mind.

This issue started with a stack of stories, essays, and poems in search of order. Boy, were they searching. One piece seemed like a natural way in: a personal essay submitted in February called "Variations on a Beginning" by a local author, M. Allen Cunningham. He'd composed it as a series of passages about boyhood and literary life, all numbered, all exploring this question of beginnings.

A natural way in, yes. The first piece. Then what?

I stared at "Variations." Hmm ... well, what if I took it apart? Could each section stand on its own? Equally crucial—would the other pieces work between?

Order emerged. Of course, it would be a futile exercise without the author's blessing. I mean, think about it. You've written this fine essay, it's been accepted for publication, and now your editor wants to turn it into a fifteen-decker sandwich. What?

I guess it's a thirteen-decker because we kept the first three "Variations" together. I'll spare you the extended food metaphor, except for this: dig in. Find out how these flavors combine. I hope you agree this is literary umami.

As you read, too, notice how each of these stories, essays, and poems begins. For instance, "No Telling" by Jody Lisberger sets up an arrival, Rosanna Staffa's "Praying In Souzhou" a goodbye. The fault lines of family extend from the poised "Two Bottles" by Chris Abbate to an impassioned "Inheritance" by Catherine Arra. The heat of New York in September, 1946, ushers in "Foot In America" by David Schultz.

Ask yourself what roused our writers to start *there*. Then look through your fonts, pick one, and conjure up a beginning of your own.

—Pam Wells

From the Publisher's Desk

I'LL NEVER FORGET THE EXPERIENCE of opening up *The New Yorker* one day back in November, 1989, to discover the entire issue taken up by a Robert Caro piece on LBJ (published in *The Years of Lyndon Johnson: Means of Ascent*). And this was only an excerpt! I'd never seen anything like it. It was riveting and I couldn't put it down.

It's easy in retrospect to say the editorial decision was the right one, because certainly there was great value in learning about this immense figure of American politics. Book I is 882 pages. Book II is 592 pages. The additional two volumes that hadn't been written yet ... add another 1,936 pages for a total read of 3,410 pages!

An actual printed book demands tactile manipulation of pages, and the words on these pages form a design. It is only by interpreting the design of the words that we form the meaning, and acquire the knowledge of those words. Three thousand, five hundred and twelve pages of meaning is a lot of knowledge, but where would all that knowledge be if not for a reader?

Writing and reading are two reciprocal parts of the knowledge sharing that we rely on for cultural continuity and, often, for discontinuity.

Reading is a ritual that takes time, to listen, to observe, to ponder, to discover. It isn't numbers, it isn't eating at the drive-in, or shopping at a strip mall. Reading is the very opposite of helter-skelter consumption.

Reading is absorbent. By reading, we come to know others, and know parts of the world beyond our own small places in it. Sometimes that takes 3,410 pages, and, astoundingly, sometimes that takes one small phrase of a poem.

Unlike flipping through the digital screens of a smartphone or tablet, reading is slow. The tempo of the mind adjusts so that knowledge can enter through the mind, sink into the body, and become understanding, or insight, or dissonance... but never simply a flip to The End.

Sustainability is a much talked about concept here in the Pacific Northwest. And reading fits right in, for readers and writers work collectively to maintain a literary culture that values knowledge. Our ability to seek and retain knowledge of another world has a direct relationship to our level of empathy and compassion.

And the more empathy and compassion we possess, the greater our understanding of the vast world we live in.

In consideration of our own future, we here at *The Timberline Review* have invited two esteemed members of the literary community to join our publication "in an advisory capacity." They have graciously agreed to lend their wisdom, experience, and favorite lunch menus to the serendipitous mix that generates *The Timberline Review* every six months.

Brian Doyle, whose writing is well known in and far beyond Portland, has offered his support to our venture from the beginning. He's a man of generous spirit and voracious talent who can't seem to stop writing stories and essays and poems. We're fortunate to count him a member of the Timberline Review Advisory Board and to include his writing as a contributing author.

And we're thrilled to welcome Per Henningsgaard to the Timberline Review Advisory Board. Per may be a relative newcomer to Portland, but he's made a powerful impact as Director of the master's degree program in Book Publishing at Portland State University and its student-staffed publishing house, Ooligan Press. Per received his PhD in 2009 from The University of Western Australia in Perth, Western Australia.

We're happy to have Brian and Per at our lunch, er, editors' table and we're confident there'll be plenty more to tell in the months ahead.

Meanwhile, we invite you to discover the Summer/Fall 2016 issue, with writing that takes you to another place, that you may find yourself there.

Sophfronia Scott's "Why I Didn't Go to the Firehouse" shares an event I think I know, but then realize it's only the big media version I know. With Sophfronia's essay, I come away with knowledge of another place and time; I come away a different person.

Words matter very much. We use words to shape our lived experience by expressing our memories and our hopes, and to learn about kindred and faraway spirits all along the way. Whatever part of the world you're in today, or wherever you might be tomorrow, thank you now for your support of our magazine.

Take time. Read. Write. Repeat.

—Peter R Field

Variations on a Beginning | M. ALLEN CUNNINGHAM

[1]

I COULD SAY AT THE OUTSET that my father stood nearly six foot eight. That for most of my boyhood he drove a potato chip truck. That his mother was a school teacher, his father the Chief of Police, that they were members of all the clubs and fraternal societies—the Masons, the Shriners, the Elks, and my favorite (they used ceremonial swords!), the Woodsmen of the World. That they were community figures in Watsonville, California, a small agricultural town on Monterey Bay, founded on a long-lost campsite of the 1769 Portola Expedition.

They lived in the red house with leaded windows and Victorian turrets on the little lane called Sudden Street. They drank and smoked themselves to death, because that was the way of life for happy, prosperous, vivacious folks in their time. My father always told us children of the hours he passed lying awake in his boyhood room listening to his parents' rattling throats, their wheezing and hacking down the hall, and vowed to himself he would never touch a cigarette.

[2]

I COULD BEGIN WITH GUNS—and not because they're unique to my story. The chromium and plastic six-shooters I wore in holsters on every errand with my mother. My grandfather's five-pound "paperweight," which was a massive black pistol encased in lead. One of several mementoes surviving from his desk at the station, it was, or so we grandkids were told, something he'd wrested from a fugitive's grip during an altercation and arrest, then had cast in lead as a souvenir. The .22-gauge rifle with which my father was shot one day in the late 1950s while playing with his sister shooting targets in the front yard, the dense black smudge of the bullet forever lodged in his shin, as he never tired of showing us, and how he would tell the story: "I came in limping saying, 'Mom, I'm shot, I'm shot, Adrienne shot me!'

and do you know what Gramma said? 'Oh, Stephen,' she said, 'stop your fooling and go back outside,' and then when she looked and saw the blood she gasped so deep she almost fainted." My father, his leg outstretched on the ottoman, his trouser cuff rolled, parts the bristling black hairs on his shin as he tells it, and my brother and I lean closer. The other .22—or was it the same gun?—that lay across the rafters in the garage, and how my brother and I got it down to play with one Saturday afternoon. We were standing in our driveway, my brother aiming it here and there and I fumbling with the box of shells, when our mother (a neighbor having called to alert her) came out to stop us.

[3]

THERE WAS ONCE A MURDER AT HEIGHTS MARKET, a mile from our house. It started with the deranged man who Mr. Heights kicked out of his store for spitting on the produce. The man returned some hours later, waited patiently in the checkout line, then shotgunned Mr. Heights point-blank in the face.

But that's a story I never heard growing up. I learned it only this year from my father, on a nostalgic drive through Watsonville.

Two Bottles | CHRIS ABBATE

Did we consider
how much depended
    on

two glass ketchup
    bottles

one on top of the other,
    mouth to mouth,

my father's curiously deft hands,
    the knots of his knuckles
    pulling away from his architecture,
    this house of cards,

and he in his furrowed work shirt,
    his chair with the cracked vinyl armrests,

the quotation marks
    of our leftover pork chop bones
    fitted together on his plate,

flecks of meat
    and a final slug of ketchup
    he would not be denied.

How very Catholic of us,
    not sinning by
    not wasting,

all that we had,
    all that we would have,
    seemed to depend on those
        two bottles,

our daily bread,
    the padding of our days,

our Rosary fingers careful
    not to upset the balance
    of the kitchen table,

Wednesday night,
    the fulcrum of the week:
    our half-finished labor,
    homework waiting in the den,
    a sitcom to watch,

and Dad at the kitchen table
    waiting on
gravity.

The Door in the River | PEPPER TRAIL

It floated, unaccountable, beneath the bridge and away downstream,
turning slowly in the current, escaped forever from its frame, leaving
a hole in some house, open to wind, the rain, to those birds and animals
and people who exist everywhere, watchful for vacancy.

I thought about the door in the river as a door, about opening it
to enter the river beneath, about that water like a photograph,
black and white, and how we think a camera is a machine, but
it is a door, that like all doors creates two worlds, outside and in.

I tried to imagine my father, as he handed me my first camera, saying
"This is a door in the river." But I could not imagine that, my father
not being given to metaphor. So instead I imagined my father and me
standing shoulder to shoulder on the bridge, watching the door float past,
each thinking his own thoughts.

A Bath in the Ganges | ROBERT HAMBURGER

AT THE SRI R.K. VENKATESWARLU ASHRAM, ardent pilgrims file past the Hindu pantheon, tranquil and unchanging, ensconced behind glass walls that shield their splendid, enchanted realms from Haridwar's dust-infused air. The faithful gaze upon Ganesh, Hanuman, Shiva, Vishnu, Brahma, Parvati, Durga, and Kali—all of them eight feet high and clothed in bright silks, resplendent in glittering costume jewelry, with mirrors and bright lights placed to enhance their divine radiance.

What, Evan wondered, were these gods made of? Nothing as substantial as wood or stone. And wax would not hold up in this heat. They must be plastic, he surmised, colossal dashboard saints. Still, he fancied them as marzipan figurines, their cloying sweetness robed in tacky artificial colors. After all, what was this ashram if not a gallery of kitschy marzipan faith? He considered himself something of an expert on this. Every Christmas, Daria set out a marzipan Nativity tableau that she'd bought at a confectioner's on one of her shopping adventures. She varnished the figures to impede their deterioration, but each year one of her cats managed to spirit off a Wise Man or a delectable barnyard creature. Daria often managed to rescue them before they'd been licked and gnawed into oblivion. Broken figures were glued together; she propped three-legged donkeys against walls and trees—but Mary's head showed signs of extensive repair, and the crèche, baby and all, bore nibble marks here and there. Daria enjoyed telling friends how the various figures met their fates; when she got on a roll, she could be animated and very funny—but he had heard these stories many times over, and marzipan no longer amused him.

Evan lingered before a glassed-in scene depicting the sacred summit of Mount Kailish. On a throne, inlaid with hundreds of mirror bits, sat Shiva—creator, destroyer, and agent of universal change. The god's smiling lips were bright red; his blue hair fell in twisting coils, and his muscled arms were cadaverous gray. A dopey-looking snake curled around Shiva's neck, and at his feet a broad ribbon of crinkled blue cellophane wriggled across the cartoon landscape.

A party of pilgrims arrived and the room filled with lively chatter. They lived with pictures of these gods in their homes; they knew the old stories and told them as bedtime tales to their children; they smeared colored paste on shrines wherever they went; they celebrated sacred history in dozens of raucous holidays; and they addressed their heavenly lords in simple prayer. Indians were a religious people; Evan knew that, yet when he witnessed displays of their unabashed devotion, he was always surprised that spectacles like this cheesy never-never land could so enthrall them.

"Ganga!" a man in a soiled *dhoti* said to him, his voice charged with wonder. He pointed at the strip of cellophane river at Shiva's feet, vivid cobalt blue, as if he was looking out upon the most glorious prospect. "Ganga! Ganga!"

Twenty minutes later, Evan joined Daria for lunch at the coffee shop in one of Haridwar's few decent hotels. They flopped into their seats, exhausted from the heat, and ordered masala omelets and fresh lime sodas. Like all proper first-class hotels, the Lakshya was air-conditioned and its windows sealed shut, creating a self-contained habitat designed to insulate intrepid voyagers from the hazards of India. There were times when Evan detested this bunker mentality, but today he welcomed the soothing isolation, the quarantine their sealed window guaranteed.

"The *arti* begins at eight," Daria said. "It's going to be wonderful!"

On a ledge on the other side of the thick glass an ant reared on its hind legs as if to force open the window. It flopped back, righted itself, and went further along, renewing its effort at a new spot. Everywhere in India outdoor life penetrated homes, temples, public buildings, every obstacle raised by man: vines grew through windows; birds, bugs, and amusing geckos came and went as they pleased. Evan indulged in a moment of whimsical indignation on behalf of the ant, denied passage that was his by natural right. Now it was scraping at the hardened putty that sealed the window in its frame.

"Foolish little ant," Daria said. "He'll never make it."

He thought of saying something. But what? Something about how their observations overlapped, how great minds think alike—but what did it count for, really? When he and Daria had begun seeing one another, they shared moments like this as signs of emotional affinity, haphazard magic tricks prepared by Fate, which they welcomed for the rush of feeling it roused. But now he was less inclined to magical thinking.

The waiter set their meal in front of them and they bolted it down in silence.

Back at the tourist lodge, Daria fell asleep instantly. It was only two o'clock, and though Evan knew he could easily will himself to sleep, he was not inclined to do so. India, he'd discovered, had the power to infuse one with an agreeable languor;

lounging about staring at nothing appeared to be a national avocation, but this afternoon he felt restless.

He rolled off the bed, careful not to disturb Daria, and stepped outside. The roof cast a strip of shadow over the balcony that served as an exterior hallway to the row of rooms. Even in the shade, it was hot and airless. Down below, barefoot boys pulled weeds from an overgrown garden. Every few minutes they abandoned their work to putter with a heap of broken flagstone, a roll of barbed wire, and a length of unconnected hose—a project that seemed to call for frequent discussion and no constructive action. Evan watched without any real curiosity.

Beyond the untended garden, a short path led down to the Ganges. At Haridwar, the river was broad and swiftly coursing with occasional whitecaps registering its descent. The churning brown water was unsightly, yet the river remained potent and imposing—a great country's great living spirit.

A stone terrace ran beside the river, broken by *ghats* that enabled people to step into the river to bathe. Evan had no faith in Ganges lore. Drinking its waters is said to have unlimited medical and spiritual benefits, and a mere dip in the river washes away the world's ills. Just the same, he decided to give it a shot—he'd bathe in the Ganges.

He headed back to his room to change into his bathing trunks. But the door didn't yield; he'd locked himself out, and he didn't want to disturb Daria by knocking. No matter—after his morning shower he had draped his towel over the balcony to dry. It was really all he needed. In the hot afternoon, there would be few people down by the river; he could go to the far end of the terrace, step out of his clothes, and bathe in his underwear without being noticed.

The balcony stairs were crowded with pots of dead plants, brittle stalks poking from useless dry soil. Only a few cactus-like things had survived, more depressing than their desiccated neighbors. He left the shabby stairwell and made his way to the *ghat*. As he approached the Ganges, a strong, incessant roar filled the air. From his perch on the balcony there had been no sound at all, but here the vast river set the torpid day in motion—as in some fairy tale when a curse is lifted to reanimate a suspended world, restoring it to life.

A solid railing, planted a few feet out in the river, ran the full length of the bathing *ghat*. Standing there, Evan felt the river's authority. The Ganges pressed downstream with tremendous force, seemingly propelled by its own urgent mission to execute the timeless drama of its Himalayan descent. A heavy tree trunk—it might have been an entire tree—bobbed fifty yards from shore; it disappeared beneath some whitecaps, then surfaced again downstream, rolling past the bathers Evan had seen from his balcony. Two young women, fully clothed in red and yellow saris, stood in the water brushing their long black hair. On the terrace, a man, probably the husband of one of the women, kneeled to snap pictures.

Evan walked away from them until he felt comfortable about stripping. He kicked off his sandals, pulled his shirt over his head, and stepped out of his pants. Then he ventured down the first step. The water was cool and the current not nearly as assertive as he'd expected. He proceeded until he was waist deep. Here the river's grip was considerably stronger and Evan braced himself by setting his legs apart. He squatted and dunked his head; then he pushed off from the steps and grabbed onto the guardrail. The river dragged at him, but he twisted onto his belly and stretched out, inviting the water to ripple over his body. Away from the shallow wash of the *ghat*, the Ganges was something to be reckoned with; it shot through him, strong and invigorating, charging him with an infinitesimal portion of its power.

He set his feet against the railing and thrust towards shore, reaching the *ghat* several feet downstream from where he'd started. He walked up a step or two and sat down. Along the opposite shore, lavish ashrams hugged the riverbank, pleasing buildings designed, he guessed, in the 1920s and painted in gentle pastels.

"Hallo! Hallo, meestair!" The greeting seemed to rise from the river itself. "You come meestair! You come!" Evan found the voice upstream. A bearded, barrel-chested man waved to him, while his other arm remained hooked securely around the railing.

Evan accepted the good-natured invitation. He stepped back into the river and lunged for the railing; he seized it and pulled himself upstream, hand over hand against the current, until the stranger reached out a muscular arm and pulled him to his spot.

"Ganga very good river," the man said. His hair was knotted in a bun on top of his head.

"Number-one river," Evan replied in the pigeon English he reserved for such occasions.

"Yes, yes, number one!" The man was pleased by his remark. "You are Inggleesh?"

"I am American."

"Very good! A-MAY-reeca number-one country. When I am getting green cart, am going a-MAY-reeca."

"India good country, too." In his three weeks of travel, Evan had said these lines so often. "Many problems. But India is good."

"I am going a-MAY-reeca. I am frand wit a-MAY-reeca." The man was all smiles. He released his knotted hair and it fell free, unraveling in wriggling coils.

Immersed in the Ganges, its strong current against his spine, Evan felt an easy fellowship with this stranger. The man was yelling something now, raising himself up on the railing and waving his arms.

"We will take peekshur. My friend ees coming."

The bathers at the far end of the terrace were on their way. The two women hung back while their companion advanced to the top of the steps.

"Nikon kemra," the man on the shore said. "You like Japanese kemra?" He did not seem interested in a reply. "Now I will make peekshur of you."

The stranger flopped a heavy arm over Evan's shoulder.

Evan regarded these moments as evidence of lingering colonial sentiment: a photo with your arm around a white man was something special. He never knew what to do—or rather, he knew what he had to do, but he didn't like it. He threw his arm over his companion's shoulder and smiled for the camera.

When it was over, he pulled away and prepared to let himself drift downstream to his original spot.

"We are bayting now," the man said.

"What?"

"Bayting! Bayting!"

Evan was completely puzzled.

"Here! Here!" The stranger picked up a bar of soap. "Dis for bayting." He began lathering Evan's chest.

"No, that's okay. Never mind." But his words made no impression.

"No problem. In Ganga, everyone bayting. A-MAY-reecan frand must do bayting."

The firm pressure of his partner's soapy hands was soothing, and Evan relaxed.

"Ganga good for you, good for me, good for everyone."

The stranger began to sing and Evan submitted to his gentle service. He closed his eyes and felt borne up by the river and by the stranger, by his generous hands and his cheerful, incomprehensible song. It had been so long since he'd been touched like this, since someone had wanted to please him with no thought of an exchange.

Evan's knotted neck muscles yielded to his companion's touch. He thought of Daria dozing up in their room. For weeks, they'd shared the intimacy of travel. He'd sat beside her in suffocating second-class railway cars for days on end, shifting bodies and luggage about to accommodate one another's cramped restlessness; they'd visited every sight together and nodded tolerantly at one another's observations; he'd watched every mouthful of food she ate; he knew when she peed and emptied her bowels, and what state her stomach was in; he'd watched her read and brush her hair and clip her toenails—intimate association, yes—familiar and private, yet, it must be admitted, numbing. It had been way too long since they'd held one another with real desire, longer still since either of them had undertaken some unilateral act of giving. To give, just give, or as in the case of this amiable stranger, to be coaxed to settle back and accept pleasure—it was so different from the companionable routine that he and Daria had settled into. Now, under this stranger's ministration, it seemed to Evan that he and Daria had tacitly agreed to settle for less than what they wanted, less than what they needed—thus ensuring that they would continue together, quietly rattling the bars of the cage that they themselves had constructed and obligingly entered, before the door slammed shut behind them.

"Thank you! Thank you very much!" he said to the stranger. He took the soap from him and prepared to rub the man's shoulders.

"No! No! No more bayting!"

"But—"

"I go now." He took his soap and climbed up to the dry terrace. "A-MAY-reeca very good. Number one." Evan watched him go—loose hair flouncing with his rolling gait.

Evan lounged on the bed while Daria dressed for the *arti*. She slipped into puffy Aladdin-like drawstring pants and an embroidered *salwar kameez* tunic top, one of several she'd bought in Lucknow. She selected her garnet necklace and the moonstone earrings she'd found in Jaipur.

Then she raised her arms and gyrated in an impromptu Bollywood dance. "Well?"

The outfit was becoming, but Evan could never quite disabuse himself of his belief that Indian clothing was meant for Indians. Even with someone as attractive as Daria there was an element of masquerade, of an ill-advised impulse that bespoke of a wish to go native. In the three weeks that he and Daria had been traveling, he'd worn an unvaried outfit of jeans, sandals, and simple short-sleeved shirts, while Daria's western clothing went untouched in the bottom of her backpack in favor of her *salwar kameezes* and one sari, which even she was forced to acknowledge 'didn't make it.' Still, she looked so carefree, so eager to immerse herself in the evening ceremony, Evan was not about to spoil the moment.

"Perfect!" he said.

They passed through the teeming market until they came to an open square where women squatted on the stone street beside sheaves of green banana leaves and mounds of marigold petals—yellow, white, and red. Deftly, they bent the leaves and tied them to form tiny hulls which they filled with handfuls of bright petals. On each of these colorful cargoes they set a tiny clay dish filled with paraffin and a strip of candlewick. Pilgrims lined up to buy them, and every child cradled one as families moved on towards the temple *ghat* where the *arti* would soon begin.

"Let's get one!" Daria said.

It was just like her, that wish to partake, to have what pleased her—to join in, or to enjoy the illusion of joining in—on occasions when he felt more comfortable standing back to observe. She was subject to bursts of enthusiastic purchases: the incredible junk she accumulated on every walk through Chinatown; the trove of cheap jewelry she snapped up in Morocco—most of it abandoned as soon as they arrived home. That camel saddle bag with its indelible, funky smell—how they lugged it through busses, trains, and airport customs only to dump it in her parents' basement. Kitschy doodads from roadside stops across America lined their win-dowsill at home; her swizzle stick collection, thrift shop clothes, and odd things she rescued at auctions. She did not really feel part of a place until she'd made an impulsive purchase—participatory consumerism, he teased. She needed to feel she was there—wherever she happened to be—to dramatize, perhaps to validate, her presence. Back in the States she'd dragged him to square dances, palm readers, huntsman dinners of inedible venison, demolition derbies, and ridiculous parades. Here in India, there were garish temples, prayer ceremonies, redundant markets, and new costumes that captured her attention.

She was happiest, she came truly alive, whenever she found some new oppor-tunity to enact her deep wish for constant transformation. This is what had drawn him to her from the very start; though back then he did not really understand it. He'd seen her as vital, adventurous, and that was enough. She was still that way—more so, perhaps, than when they'd first met—but it was no longer the same. Or maybe he was no longer the same. At the start, he'd had no way of anticipating what it might be like actually living with her, living with that restlessness. A karma chameleon. But this was who she'd been from the start. To say she'd changed was unfair. Her hunger for new selves was an unchanging part of her.

These thoughts did not come to him in so many words. But they were there, triggered by her impulse to buy one of those simple leaf vessels. Had he been alone he would never have bought one. But he was not alone; if he had been, he might never have come to India.

They joined the burgeoning crowd as it shuffled down to the river. A hodge-podge of small temple buildings formed a small courtyard that opened to bleacher-like *ghat*s. Off to one side, a broad bridge connected the mainland to an islet fifty yards from shore. The isle was flat, completely paved, with rows of steps that faced the temple *ghat*s on shore. Already, hundreds of people had gathered there, while others leaned out from the bridge railing. He and Daria joined the pilgrims on the little island and found places to sit on the warm stone.

Dusk fell and the massed buildings of Haridwar turned gray and insubstantial. Lights blinked in shops and homes, as the buildings themselves disappeared entirely. In the indistinct light, Evan was aware of bodies moving, pressing together in a living chain, as though some benign river creature had risen to stretch its immense body in the welcoming darkness.

On shore, boys stripped to their undershorts and dove into the river. Arms flailing, they battled the Ganges with frenzied windmill strokes until they reached Evan's island fifty yards downstream. But one boy failed to make it. He dog-paddled feebly and then submitted as the strong current swept him away.

Evan felt a wave of alarm. For an instant, he thought of diving in to attempt a rescue, but he knew the river would overpower him. Then, as the helpless boy hurtled under the bridge, his fatal passage ended abruptly—his hands clutched empty air and he soared free of the river, his body ascending miraculously into the night. For an instant, Evan allowed himself to imagine that one of the great Hindu gods he'd seen that morning at the ashram had intervened to call the boy heavenward. But in a moment an explanation presented itself: ropes dangled from the bridge; the boy had grabbed one and was shinnying up to the railing—followed by more boys—in what, it was now clear, was a popular test of youthful prowess.

Along the *ghat*s, several people touched matches to the wicks on their banana-leaf boats. Then they set their delicate vessels in the river, lights aflicker, and let them go. The crafts spun and bobbed, then surrendered to the current that bore them away.

The boys in the river waded along the *ghat*s helping to launch the leaf boats. Each boy cradled a few in his arms and kicked out in the water to set them free. Evan adjusted the vessel in his lap. He lit a match and held it to the wick.

"Not yet," Daria said. "It's not time."

"What does it matter?" he said. But he knew that it did matter, it mattered to her, for whatever reason. "Here!" He dropped the boat in her lap. "It's yours."

A great clanging arose from the temple, accompanied by music from blaring speakers. Priests appeared, each one bearing what looked like a tiered chandelier. Someone hurried about handing flaming torches to the priests—the chandeliers burst into flame and the dark river glowed with jagging orange light.

Now, hundreds of matches flared as pilgrims launched their boats—a sparkling flotilla, bumping, bobbing, and snagging, but rarely capsizing. Daria borrowed a light from a stranger. When the wick was lit, she set their hull on the river and let it go.

Evan stared at the spectacle: fragile crafts illumined by winking lights, drawn into the maw of immense darkness. Near the bridge the flotilla disappeared behind a promontory, then reemerged further downstream—delicate, ephemeral, a swarm of fireflies.

"A holy river," Evan said.

"Yes, of course it is."

"It's like—"

"Shhhh. . ." She seized his hand.

Flaming lamps and gleaming candles cast a golden light over Daria's face. Her eyes were wide, her lips parted as if even the slightest breath would break the spell. She surrendered to the moment in a way he knew he never could. It was ridiculous, he was tempted to tell her, ridiculous to imagine that you can pretend you're Indian. Your *salwar kameez* and all those trinkets don't change anything. You're you. You're not one of them.

She stroked his hand. "It's beautiful, isn't it?"

"Yes," he replied, "beautiful . . ." He looked down at their fingers twined together.

They joined the pilgrims filing back across the darkened bridge: pressed close, shuffling patiently. Along the shore, the evening market sprang to life, bustling with photographers, musicians, wouldbe guides, and beggars. Fried breads and snacks sizzled in pans of hot oil. Hawkers spread blankets on the stone street to sell garlands, souvenir scarves, cheap jewelry, and religious keepsakes.

A line of people in soiled garments blocked their path, milling in place with empty, bone-tired faces, the deep fatigue of poverty. Temple priests distributed banana leaves to each weary pilgrim, followed by generous dollops of rice and dal. When they finished eating, they curled up and went to sleep on the stones. Hunger had simplified their lives.

Nearby, a boy with no arms sat on the street sketching pictures with his toes. He was shirtless, a saffron *dhoti* tied about his waist, colored pens by his side. His drawings were surprisingly good: familiar scenes of Rama, Ganesh, Durga, Shiva, and Parvati, rendered with dreamlike fluency. The boy held the pen between his first two toes, controlling the instrument so easily that Evan momentarily forgot he was not simply using his hands. The young artist concentrated on his work, paying no attention to the small crowd.

Passersby tossed small coins onto the boy's blanket. Evan pulled a hundred-rupee note from his pocket and slipped it under the blanket, just beside the boy's leg, leaving an edge exposed where the boy could not miss seeing the relatively lavish gift. But the boy did nothing to acknowledge Evan's largesse. He was at work on Shiva, limning a Himalayan landscape in the background. He exchanged his green pen for a blue one and began to draw a band of river.

"Let's buy it!" Daria said.

"I just gave him one hundred rupees!" A few days earlier, she had reproached him for giving what she felt to be a stingy tip, yet now she seemed indifferent to his charitable act.

"That was a gift."

"He didn't even look up!"

"He's working."

"For one hundred rupees he could nod his head."

"If it's a gift he shouldn't have to do anything."

He was tired of their trifling quarrels, tired of how petty they made him feel. While Daria paid for the drawing, he wandered back to the riverbank and peered into the dark water hoping to see one last glowing vessel. He had bathed in the Ganges and in some way he felt invested in their passage—but the vessels were gone.

Still, in his mind's eye he saw the blind flotilla traveling in darkness, rudderless barques brushing and bumping helplessly in the night—fragile, yet just sturdy enough to stay afloat. Downstream, he knew, lay Varanasi, the portal to new life, where people proffered loved ones to the burning *ghat*s, entrusting their remains to the living river. From there, human ashes and stubborn charred limbs would join the fleet of leaves and petals, his little hull amongst them. Laden with this solemn cargo, the Ganges gathers detritus from myriad cities and villages, as well as disintegrating clay effigies of the gods, uprooted trees, and countless marigold garlands, all mingling in a ceaseless, sacred procession through baking plains, disbanding at last in an alluvial delta, where the great river breaks and sprawls in an ever-changing labyrinth—a thousand weary fingers, reaching, reaching for the open sea.

Variations on a Beginning | M. ALLEN CUNNINGHAM

[4]

THERE ARE MANY STARTING POINTS, IT SEEMS—memories and anecdotes shaken loose from the narrative I or my folk have constructed, pieces that don't seem to fit in any one place. For instance, some years ago, my mysterious inability to wear a watch. How the hands would come loose and swing about the dial. Three different watches I tried and, one after the other, returned them all, defective. Always the hands were fixed when I bought a watch, adrift once I'd worn it a day or so.

This, of course, is not a story but merely something that happened, which is different. And I might tell how this mystery passed, how, eventually, I could wear a watch again (I wear one now), but this is not the same thing as a story's end.

Are we rooted in stories, narratives, anecdotes, or something else? A loose and airy soil. A depository for oddments of all kinds. How do we begin to tell where we came from? The things that shaped us, or seemed to.

The Eel Catcher | ANN E. MICHAEL

I was only nine when I caught the eel, in a lake
I think, yet I remember well the force as it
yanked, the pole jittering in my hands, a gyroscopic
frenzy.
I yelled something, and a man—it might
have been my father—clasped his large hands
around my fists, guiding and reeling in
the line. The eel flailed,
its whip-dark body so riled with fight
I thought I'd snared some kind of monster
but I released my pole to the adults only after the whirled
impetus of that serpentine fish nearly knocked me
off the pier.
Someone wrangled the eel to the planking.
I'd have let it go if it had stayed
motionless for even a moment, long enough
to untwist the hook from its
serrated mouth. One of the men—
it wasn't my father—
bashed its head. A sleek stillness
overtook the writhing and the body lay
like an inked scribble, sinuous
on the dock, sheen-scaled, slate-
colored, a failed fish I had not landed on my own.
Back to the shore I walked to pick up stones
and skim them along the water's surface. The men
stayed on the pier. They did not notice
me noticing the distance between us or
the judder and slink of the eel's
wild nerves.
I would have let it go.

On A Deschutes County Road in Winter

| DAVID MELVILLE

Crossing that open country where mountains row up
like chorus girls, they each stood large on my road

this one sheer, the next cragged, the next slim bottomed, another
broad faced, another red topped, an elegant plump. With each

curve I traversed, skirting the troublesome faces and giving
wide berth to knife edges, admiring wild legs and canyons,

the wind shifted. Cloud boas dangled from fir shoulders, then fluttered off,
feather white. And I was twelve again, stiff with the prospect

of the slow dance and the cold sweat that accompanied
palms at basement parties cupped around a bony waist.

Revelation happens like that, in burlesque moments,
a grope for contact we want but are afraid to touch.

Then I knew it like my Ford pickup's ripped upholstery,
how, as night dropped its black negligee, somewhere

in the distance another would queue up, waiting to dance.

We Were Always the Good | CLARA MAE BARNHART

Cousin Michelle used to catch crayfish, feed
them salamanders and make them fight to the
death at family picnics at Martin Brook Park.
We swam in the deep section by the drainage
spout and waded through the murky water
under the old stone bridge.
We stuck our heads up hollow trees
and howled and yipped like a pack of coyotes,
cut trails through posted property and sprinted
through pricker patches, streaks of blood left bare
for the flies on our forearms.
We pretended to be orphans after we ate
the hotdogs our parents had prepared for us,
found patches of moss to lay our heads on,
pretending to wake up from a dream with a start,
a ragtag troupe of us on the run from the bad guys.
We were always the good.
Cousin Dorothy's red hair was too long and tangled,
she had buck teeth and would only wear socks
that were two sizes too big, they sagged limp
around her ankles and slid down into her shoes.
She often played the part of the kid who got
captured and had to sit quietly
somewhere and hide until we found her.
Cousin Curt threw pennies at us, hard
when we weren't looking.
Nick cried when he lost.
Andy always held the littlest one's hand
so that they didn't trip over roots
when we played man-hunt in the night.
Billy wore glasses and was thirty-four pounds
on his ninth birthday.
Quinn got freckles on his nose every summer
and always fell asleep with his head on my shoulder
in the back of the minivan.

We locked him out of the room when we were
playing the characters in our girl pretend games
that he wouldn't understand.
Hot tears on his cheeks while he kicked the door.
Cousin Emily collected wildflowers and pressed
them between the pages of overdue library books.
She sent me letters through the mail
that she wrote in calligraphy.
We lived twelve miles apart.
Once she wrote: calligraphy is fun,
but it is very meticulous.
We took piano lessons back, to back, to back,
every Friday after school with Mrs. Sim
in the Presbyterian Church on Main Street.
While one of us was earning a star, or
a scolding so gentle that it resembled a yawn,
the rest of us played in the Sunday school room.
We drew pictures and wrote messages
on the chalk board that were never about god but
that we left like secret codes hoping someone
would see them signed, Love Jesus, or
Santa Claus, and believe it.

Lost Boy: Peter Pan's Mother Has Her Say

| BRITTNEY CORRIGAN

Flight isn't actually born of happy thoughts,
no matter what he'd have you think. It's like
two magnets that repel: so similar, they fly
from each other if they come too close.
That's how he learned to star-step:
we began to rub against each other
like tinder and flint, sparks flung aloft
and his body buoyed up by the heat.
He told you he fell from his pram?
That I closed the window? Listen,
it wasn't that simple. Doesn't every boy
sit up in the dark and call out from his dreams?

He says he doesn't need a mother, yet
he's drawn to countless mothering things.
They all want to tend him.
Take the fairy. She knows she can't seduce,
so instead she claims him. She protects,
jealousy lighting her from within, so bright
it's audible. She warns. She lays down
her life in front of his. Or the mermaids,
their fishy bodies draped across his lap, raising
and lowering their eyelids like chum to draw
him up and out. But I ask you, where are they
when the tide comes in? When he puffs out
his chest and the water crests his heels?

And the Never bird—what kind of mother
is she—offering her floating nest
for rescue when the mermaids abandoned
him in the middle of their kelp-stink
lagoon? All those days adrift with her
passenger eggs, feathers spread to shelter
them from the sun, long neck stretched up

and out to threaten the rain—how could
she trust my wild and crowing boy
with their two fragile forms? What if
the tarpaulin hat had not been at hand
to receive them? Would he have left
the eggs on the wave-drenched rock
and sailed back to his rowdy den of boys?

Then there's Wendy. All shadow-stitching,
medicine, and stories, playing at motherhood
as if it could give her wings. Stroking my boy's
hair when the night terrors take him. Pressing
his head full of baby teeth into her nightdress,
thimble-kisses falling from his pockets and rolling
across the earthy, root-torn floor. He pretends
not to need any of them, but his dreams turn him
inside out, hook-handed and savaged, while
my window shutters bang against the house, rain
soaking the bedclothes, curtains flapping
like the sails of a shipwreck as the last
of the pirates burble and siphon down.

Who says I can tidy his mind?
Smooth out his dreams?
A mother is just another kind of shadow.
A mother is just another kind of star.
But for now, he is sleeping. I can wander
my fingers through his hair and spy
on his dreams. I cannot tame them.
I cannot stitch him back to me
when the nightmares come. Sweet boy,
tonight I've left the window open.
You can fly, my darling. You can fly.

In My Defense | BRIAN DOYLE

I GRASPED THE CONCEPT OF PLAYING DEFENSE on a basketball court from the very start of my motley career; I understood the straightforward principles, I admired the simplicity of the basic premise, that you should stay near your man at all times, ideally between him and the basket, while remaining alert and aware of the ball's movement, and the ever-present possibility of picks being set behind and around you; I even quickly apprehended the intricacies of shifting zone defenses, the swift calculus of the one-two-two, the box-and-one, the triangle-and-two, the half-court trap, the full-court press; all this I understood, and even enjoyed in theory, much as I loved chess and its endless thrust and counter-thrust and ever-shifting patterns; it was lovely to think about how one team might defend a team with a single great shooter, or how you could neutralize another team's greater height, or how you could pack the lane and force a poor-shooting team to try their luck from the arctic regions. The problem for me, though, was that actually playing defense was deeply and unendurably boring, and I could never last more than a few seconds before trying to enliven matters by stealing the ball, or abandoning my man to crash a pick, or abandoning my man to sag down on a big guy who was foolishly bringing the ball down below his waist, where us munchkins could swipe at it. Why big guys always wanted to dribble is a mystery to me, but they did, and still do, the poor lumbering mastodons.

I think every coach I ever had sat me down at one point and gave me a speech that went something like this: Son, you are a decent athlete, and you are not a complete idiot, and you appear to understand the basic principle of the two defenses we play, we do not play fifty defenses, we only play two, and they are fairly straightforward in their basic premises, which is to say that a man-to-man means that you stay with your man, and a zone means that you stay in your assigned region of the court, but you do not stay with your man, but range about free as a bird, defending no one in particular and going for steals and blocks even though I have asked you one thousand times not to do that, and when we switch to zone you do not stay in your region, but gambol about loose and free, letting your man sit in his rocking chair and drill short uncontested shots all game long, which is giving me gray hair and ulcers, and can you explain why you are so uninterested in any hint or iota of defense? Not to mention that you often do not seem to get the signal from our point guard that we are switching from one defense to another. It is a fairly simple signal, don't you think, a closed fist? Yet you seem to cheerfully set up in whatever defense you think we are in, and then abandon even the appearance of playing that defense, and set about your headlong free-form journeys and voyages. Could you possibly explain to me what, if anything, you are thinking about any of this? Son?

But it was hard for me to articulate my feelings about defense, which were complex. First, it was deadly boring to dog just one opponent for long minutes at a time, when there were so very many to swipe at and collide with and exchange vulgar pleasantries with; why defend only one man thoroughly, when you could swipe ineffectually at all five? Second, the first rule of orthodox defense was to stare intently at your man's chest, avoiding looking him in his shifty eyes, ignoring his feints and fakes, all the while doing your utmost to legally interrupt his progress, but all of this sensible stuff, in my view, ignored the thrilling fact that the ball was right there to be taken, as alluring a gleaming object as you could imagine, and who would not make a concerted effort to steal such a valuable thing, if you could? Third, what could possibly be cooler than blocking a shot, anyone's shot, so that if a guy ten feet away was lining up a shot, why should I not take a stab at it, whether or not the shooter then instantly delivered the ball to my man for an easy layup, which happened one million times, causing our coach to make that strangled sound in his throat like he was having trouble swallowing a badger?

Fourth, it seemed to me that coaches and point guards put an unseemly emphasis on stopping the other team from scoring, when a much more attractive and entertaining approach was to simply outscore the other team. In my view, if I gave up twenty points to the guy I was supposed to be covering on defense, but scored more than twenty myself, I was up on the deal, and I think I am in an unassailable position here, for if we all outscored our guys, we would have more points, and we would win the game, and the coach would not make that strangled sound in his throat as if he had just eaten a kitten-and-mayonnaise sandwich, a sound I knew all too well.

There are many adjectives you could use to describe me as a defender, ranging from lazy to terrible to ridiculous to hilarious to abject to irresponsible to hapless to ludicrous to lunatic, and I am the first to acknowledge that all those adjectives are uncomfortably accurate, but I still maintain that no one ever had more sheer fun playing defense than I did, swiping constantly for steals and constantly earning fouls (you are allowed five, so why not use your entire allowance?), trying to block any shot within the metro area, calling to my teammates to cover my man for me when I lost track of his whereabouts, and other pleasurable things like that. It still makes me smile to remember the way I would cheerfully wave at my teammates and call their attention to my man, as he sailed unobstructed to the basket, and they would gesture back at me animatedly, in those subtle but eloquent signals that ballplayers use when words fail them, and the coach would make that strangled sound in his throat, as if he had just eaten a particularly large fried chipmunk, when he thought he had ordered the smaller snack-sized one, with chips and pickles on the side.

Variations on a Beginning | M. ALLEN CUNNINGHAM

[5]

I COULD BEGIN WITH NAMES. Of places. Of loved ones. (And must I change the loved ones' names on paper? Well, you've already met my father.) So, names.

Allen, my middle name, derives from old Vermont, or so the family story goes—the name is an ancient ligature to that colonial figure (a character in many stories himself) Ethan Allen, of the Green Mountain Boys, the militia whose members were sure they could capture Montreal. As a middle name I share it with my great-grandfather Ernest Kurzweil, a skilled gardener who lived to be ninety-six, who fought in the Great War in France (I've inherited his pocket map of Paris), whose life was saved because he knew how to make gravy (and was transferred from common soldier to cook), whose people, in his mother's line, were Wenzel, a family that enjoyed a minor dynasty in Prague where, in the last decades of the nineteenth-century, one of them became related to Rainer Maria Rilke by marriage, something wholly unknown to me until I'd been writing a book about Rilke for years.

Or the name Robley, as the family of my great-grandmother Avis was called, and the winding country track outside Monterey—still called Robley Road—in that gorgeous, distinctively Northern California valley known as the Corral de Tierra, which Steinbeck dubbed The Pastures of Heaven in his book of that title.

Or, while I am following the names in this way, I could tell of old Mrs. Rodgers, whose maiden name was Steinbeck, and who was known in Watsonville to be the author's aged sister, and how she lived with her husband in the great white farmhouse on a one-acre plot which was all that remained of the farm, while in the asphalt lot next door (the shopping center called East Lake Village) stood Lambert's Market where my father worked, a long yellow apron draped over his shirt and tie, and a pricing gun always at hand, and how he would carry over, once a week, old Mrs. Rodgers' standing order of groceries and think, The famous author's sister, how 'bout that.

I could then mention, again, that recent nostalgic drive with my father through town, and how we found the old farm lot empty, a barren scrubland of weeds, and the grand white house gone, torn down for reasons we couldn't know.

Nomenclature | ANDREA HOLLANDER

In the forest where I used to live,
birds peopled the air with conversation
I could not decipher
any more than the gibber on a train
through Kazakhstan.
Vulture or hawk, nuthatch or finch,
I didn't know which song was which.

I, who can distinguish
iambic from trochaic, who can't
not distinguish them, even
in ordinary speech, chose
not to identify birds by their calls.
I wanted my forest walks
unburdened by knowledge.

Where else can the mind let go?
Where else can the breath
be only breath and pass through us
with necessary inattention?

My father liked knowing
that a certain screech is a finch's
mating call and not a sparrow's
alarm. Near the end, when he no longer
remembered anyone's name,
he made sounds
at least his wife could understand.

I wasn't there. I was walking
in the forest, my breath steady,
my thoughts as empty
as the forest would allow.

If there were flickers
busying the branches,
they paid me no mind.
They no longer offered
whatever words
they once had for me,
a creature
they'd grown so used to
I could have been
a wood pile. I could have been
a weed.

The Apricot Tree | RICHARD SPILMAN

Moving In

The movers are late, so you sleep on a couch
you found perched curbside near a burned out
house, smelling just slightly of smoke and beer,
and in the morning like a bit of leftover night,
down the stairs she comes, the neighbor above,
with mail that somehow preceded you—
her body almost pure line like a wave.

You introduce yourself, exiled from the City
when the market's fall swallowed so many.
Befuddled by beauty, you relate the dream
that woke you: your couch flying on the back
of a carp—you don't know one fish from another,
but words appear in the dumb show of your
dreams. She offered her hand and her name.

Interpreting Dreams

Later, the furniture settled, your flat
resembling the one you had fled, and her,
on that same couch, legs gathered beneath,
you relate another dream: you in an unfinished
house, framed but open like whale ribs
picked clean on the beach, and your ex
in the yard wanting answers—to what?—
calling your name as your mother
did when you were small and late
for dinner, searching the spectral house,
though you stood there in plain sight.

She said she never remembered dreams
but knew about feeling unseen. A man
she'd loved had sailed off months ago
on a catamaran, leaving the usual note
with generic reproaches and apologies.
"After he disappeared, so did I."
When things were good he'd taught her
on a ten foot skiff. She missed that more
than the man, taut rope in her hands, leaning,
into the wind as they arced over the Bay,
dangling, as the gunwale skipped the waves.

What Love Leaves Behind

She brought gifts to people she liked,
and though the two of you seldom met,
she gave you shells from the beach,
an old edition of Peterson's Guide.
For her lover she'd made of papier mache
a blue kangaroo, alluding to a movie

they'd liked. When he took a hike
she left it by the fence near the trash
where from her kitchen window
she could watch it moulder in the rain:
the blue skin pocked with white ulcers,
the wire tail a cage full of scraps.

This, you think, is how love dies,
not like the dropping of a curtain
or the turning of a corner, but in this
slow erosion watched from a window
by a woman who cannot hate
or forgive or let go her pain.

The Names of Things

Once, you drove to a salt marsh
where shore birds tiptoed over
the oscillating waves, stabbing
their scythes into the sand.

You shared her binoculars—
a curlew, she said, female,
a whimbrel, male. All you saw
were thin-legged brown birds
nervously dipping and dipping,
their thin legs often at odds with
the weight of their plump bodies.
As with calculus, you pretended

to understand, looked for shortcuts,
but could feel her interest fading
like a dream in the light of dawn.
Curlew, she said, avocet, stilt.

Apricot Tree

In the spring the two of you
planted tomatoes, squash and beans,
watermelons from a pack of pale seeds.
The beans curled in defeat,
the tomatoes offered miniatures,
and the squash conquered the yard,
fat green zucchinis so numerous
you couldn't eat them fast enough.
The melons, after a promising start
turned yellow, then orange—
pumpkins! How could you or any
damned fool make that mistake?
You blamed each other and drank
to the confounding of every plan.

Meanwhile, in its corner, the crooked
apricot by the drive proffered
its white buds and green fruit without
your help or interest, and even
when they warmed to yellow rocks
you suspected a scam—apples?
After they flamed and softened
you tried a few. Juice (from apricots!)
sprayed your faces, stained your shirts.
No store fruit had prepared you
for this burst of untended joy.
You ate yourselves sick and made
friendly love, sticky with a ripening
you'd done nothing to deserve.

Lessons in Picking Fruit | PETER SERCHUK

1

With peaches, women do it best.
Or a man who's learned from gentleness
a sweeter thing may come. You start
with open palm, as if gravity's smallest
soul had lighted on the hand. Only then
do fingers close, barely resting on
the globe, and a gentle tug as if bringing
your only child into the world.

2

For pears, bring strong legs,
a stubborn back, and a ladder sure as
any friend. Each load is 30 pounds,
basket after basket, up and down
all day. The sap's like glue, every insect
loves your eyes and despises something
human size thieving in their world.
After a day of pears, you'll have earned
your rest; your meal, your bath
and a few cold beers.

3

Now cherries are like poodles,
high strung and full of need. But once
they've swelled into their sweetness,
fingers learn the hard way they don't
wish to leave their tree. The stems
are like barbed wire when you pull
the clusters clean; wounds every man
forgets once the sweet pit curls his tongue.

After the Blizzard | EMILY RANSDELL

for Hannah

We had yet to learn what loss was.
We hadn't seen its ruins, the passenger seat
soaked despite towels, everything smelling
the way metal tastes in the mouth.

For us, the worst storm in decades
was a lovebirds' adventure in a rented
farmhouse where across the road, bare limbs
of redbud would astonish us come spring.

Three days after, sky finally brightening,
we woke to find the white yard surrendered,
fenceline trampled by drifts, horizon risen
to the sills. We stood eye to eye with the frozen
cardinal who must have waited days
for his morning breadcrumbs,
red wings splayed.

Cistern frozen,
cabinets fouled by field mice,
we flushed the toilet with snowmelt and stacked
the counters with dishes happily left undone.
Wind spit nails at the windows but for us
it simply meant more time to lie together,
our home-sewn curtains closed.

We counted the days till spring the way later
we counted weeks, then months, all the seasons
that would pass with the same finality:
unviable, the procedures that would fail
and fail again to bring you forth.

We had yet to learn how sorrows too
would call out to be counted, how the dark
clouds of their kind would gather like birds
heavying the thicket before snow.

So many winters before your father
would finally sit at my bedside, counting aloud
as I labored, a blessed distraction as that last
storm moved through me, its clean white blanket
covering everything that had happened
before you found your way to your name.

Variations on a Beginning | M. ALLEN CUNNINGHAM

[6]

THE ORDER OF EVENTS, I'VE LONG BELIEVED, is not so important. The truth is much larger than chronology, and sequence alone, convincing as it may be, can serve to explain in only the most specious way. Because the truth is (isn't it?) that so little can stand on explanation. What joins our days together into a lived experience is not the linear, calendric, forward march of hours, months, years, and epochs which, for the sake of civilization, orders time for us by our consent. What joins our days together into a lived experience is, more truthfully, a vague webwork, a gossamer of associations, memories, and sensations. However much we claim to believe in a standardized chronology of event, this gossamer remains central to who and what we are. Manifesting the insubstantial evidence of our lives, it permits very little elaboration or embellishment from the rational linear world. Adhering to the skeleton of memory, it catches everything—or everything important—storing impressions we rarely understand at first, but like a language as one learns it these impressions accrete meaning over time.

"When you write," said Edmond Jabes, "you do not know whether you are obeying the moment or eternity." Isn't that also a description of what it's like to be alive, to possess consciousness and memory?

"In practical life, time is a form of wealth with which we are stingy," said Italo Calvino. "In literature, time is a form of wealth to be spent at leisure and with detachment."

And yet there's the rigid demand placed on writers today: that they "sell" their stories to the reader, beginning with Page One and continuing with every page thereafter. Always a forward march.

I'm not unaware of this demand. But oh, the perverseness: expecting little from the writer beyond manipulation, little from the reader beyond passivity.

Dear Reader, How about this: I sell you nothing (selling is a publisher's business). What you read here is freely given: my consciousness to yours. And may your reading be something like the Zen experience Master Shunryu Suzuki-Roshi describes:

> It is not like going out in a shower in which you know when you get wet. In a fog, you do not know you are getting wet, but as you keep walking you get wet little by little.

Just South of the Bixby Canyon Bridge | TRAVIS TRUAX

I stood alone
along the coast
like men stand
at other men's funerals.
Fog-silent
in the inner margins
of memory.
Waves, like years
broke and fell.
I bent the wind
with my hand,
marked the rough
rocks
with a stick
to silently say
there is no
place I have been
that I have not
in many ways,
loved. Each woven
home I've kept
was born
of silent fathers
and mothers
who stole away
the silence
with song. I have
carried the ocean
across Kansas
and I came back
lighter, now
that the coast
is done swimming
against me. Salt air

and grey land
make men glad
there is space
memory can't
move through. Blank
forgiveness
fills the end
without demand,
and no trail west
forgets
where it began.

To My Parents on their Separation | CHRIS ABBATE

Let's call it
a forty-seven year itch
a pothole
a cosmic zephyr.

Let's call it
a phase
a stage.

Let's agree to disagree.

Let's say love
is a braiding of synapses
an orgy of neurons
and marriage
is a chemistry experiment
in need of a slight tweak
every decade or so.

Let's rewind the tape
to the day you met
the snowy hill
his toboggan
your teenage clothes
a jealous expectation
the audacity of hormones.

Let's say what followed
the cooking and laboring
the bearing and abiding
even the nights sleeping
were stones across a river
a wooden footbridge
half-steps up a mountain.

Let's say your vows
were self-evident
an unconscious duty
an invisible hinge
an insistence of sparrows
nesting in a trellis
in early March
they only know
how to build.

The Turnover | PAULANN PETERSEN

In this game a husband and wife are not
necessarily a team. This time, the husband, his wife,
and the wife's dearest friend each have other partners.
Here, the three compete.
The teams begin
on even ground, but before the wife has even
touched her pencil to paper, the best friend
draws a few sure lines, then turns what she's drawn
upside down. Her partner looks and says,
"Capsize!" It's done.

                   In mere seconds
the best friend has sketched the cup of a boat,
its mast and sail, the waving line of water.
Then, with a simple reversal,
she's won.

            From the husband's voice comes
the cry of the best friend's name,
its three syllables singing a whole refrain
of *How could anyone be so/ clever*
doesn't begin to describe/ you really are/ my god
you are/ wonderful—a sound that rushes
in less than a heartbeat from him to her
to him, then into the high color
flooding the best friend's
delighted face.

            The dazed wife applauds—
wondering why she didn't think of it first.
How could she miss a thing so obvious,
been so easily outdone? Yet she has to give
this wonderful friend her due: it is
a perfect clue.

            Most any fool but the wife
sees by now this is *m'aidez, m'aidez*—

the boat's tipped over and everyone's headed
into the water. Arms churn, legs pump.
The wife chokes and flails, goes under
and under, rises to glimpse the husband taking
steady determined strokes. Right beside him,
the dear best friend—even as she swims—
is still smiling, her face slick and shining,
knowing herself to be more than game.
She and the husband are
a team.
       They'll right themselves.
                       In no time.

Joe's Daughter | PETER SERCHUK

Joe wants me to marry his daughter
but he doesn't know the kind of man I am.
She is sweet like the cherry wine Norwegians
sip at Christmas and I am the bitter grinds of
yesterday's coffee. She tells me she loves me,
again and again, parading the terror of her
gentleness through my imagination. I fear
it's the bitterness she loves but each time
I warn her she takes off her clothes.
Her skin smells like hay after summer rain,
waking every creature in the field.

Joe wants me to marry his daughter
but he doesn't know the kind of man I am.
I come from a good family, so he assumes I am good.
I read books by wise men, so he assumes I am wise.
I say kind things in his house, so he assumes I am kind.
But the rain is good, miles from the hurricane.
And the saint is wise, miles from temptation.
And the witch is kind while she heats the oven.
When I tell this to his daughter, she bites my ear
and sings like the finch in our tree.

Joe wants me to marry his daughter
but he doesn't know the kind of man I am.
His faith's too whole for this cracked-egg world,
proclaiming each day more right than not.
He likes to dance across a room like Fred Astaire.
When I speak of all the armies I've deserted, he fills
my glass and calls me a patriot. A man can only take
so much of praise. Little wonder I begin to wonder
if he's right. Have I underestimated the elasticity
of the soul? Can a man morph into another man
better than the man he knows? Maybe just the man

to marry his precious daughter, that silky caterpillar
with a hundred loving arms. I'd have to watch my step,
love's such a slippery ledge and she's wild and free
as any shooting star. Yet sweet like the cherry wine
Norwegians drink at Christmas. And mad enough
to taste something sweet in bitter grinds.

Doubt | ANDREA HOLLANDER

It's like that coat he wore
that seemed to usher the storm
into the house even after he removed it—
his wool and cashmere coat,
its fur-lined collar and cuffs made
to keep out the cold.
                              Icy air
entered the house with him,
spreading its molecules of bitterness
into the room, its molecules
of indifference. Even wearing
her flannel nightgown
beneath her thick robe, knee socks
and slippers, she shivered a little.

Inheritance | CATHERINE ARRA

I.

Momma's breasts were dry.
She took the shot that stopped the flow.
She bought the formula and bottled it.
The 1950s. Dr. Spock said so
and I suckled a hunger that's grown
ever since.

II.

Daddy, he noticed when my breasts swelled
and my smell changed. He hightailed it
out of there and left me to you.
But you Momma, you ignored it all
waved it off as the inevitable other arm
of every woman's cross.
I bled into my panties, a rich red jewel
circled fingertips around caramel nipples.
I swallowed Daddy's terror
grew into a woman
while you remained a girl.

III.

The first half of my life
I lived underground. He sent me there
the first time I crawled into pots and pans
upsetting a closeted order. Again, when I uttered
first refusals of peas and bedtimes.
Every time I ventured up out of dirt, reaching
to clasp long fingered light.
I'd inch my head above the surface

wrestle forearms into the grassy carpet.
In horrible delight, I'd summon the courage
to reveal my face, lift my haunches and
steady trembling legs until
his shadow came like the great beanstalk giant.
You never stepped between, stopped his rage.
I learned to live in darkness as Persephone did
without you.

IV.

It's a thankless job, she said,
from my mother before me, to hers before her
right on back to the crones banking my genetic shores.
I'm drowning in their memory of having drowned
and resurrecting on forcep steel.
It's time to say *Ciao* my child, I wish you well
and wield everyday spring in spite of you.
I despise these winters and more, the bold bragging of fall.
You ate the damn pomegranate seeds, boasted they were sweet,
left me alone to darn socks and cultivate wheat.
Did you ever think that I too may dream of silt and darkness
and a lover who unfolds?

V.

When I need you, Daddy
I need jazz. Sassy swing dancing to *Autumn Leaves*.
We hit every accent because you lead, remembering
your drumming days. How slick and sexy those sticks,
backbone slouched over Gretsch skins.
I your little girl, one and only
before breasts and body hair.
I fell in love in the jazz place, Daddy
and am faithful still.
From here I back step and strut
spinning to the beat of a middle class gig.
You gave me the rhythms I'd live by

when you played. I mean jazz
when you played jazz.

VI.

I am my father's daughter
the firm, moist flesh under the foreskin
the blood-jet urge rising to discover a mystery
to hold it in cupped palms, a moment
before it flees.
I was three, maybe four years old
creeping into the bathroom, sneaking up
under the old footed tub.
You pretended innocence when I peeked over the edge
steam curling from your shoulders
water glistening on olive skin.
I squealed a triumphant giggle over your "Oh!"
and propped myself on the porcelain rim.
It was the first and last time I touched
your soft sex, alive and white
a curious sea creature floating beneath
the surface in a tangle of silk.
I don't recall what we talked about
as you lathered and soaked, nor do I know
when we stopped talking altogether.

The woman now, looks back
through her mother's eyes
and knows why she chose you
your volcanic temper
and boyish charm, as overpowering, seductive
as her father's forbidden reach, the silent thief.
How could you know?
she didn't know, didn't want to or couldn't.
It's a man's violence and
she honored it.
But when she thought you liked me better,
I lost her.

VII.

All the men, or were they boys,
I chose, the two I married;
they weren't Daddy.
They were you Momma, in every tenderness
you couldn't offer, curled up and away in the same void
the same vacuous silence, the blank shock
death at ground zero, before speech
before the tiny bud of spirit could wink and flower.

Variations on a Beginning | M. ALLEN CUNNINGHAM

[7]

BUT NARRATIVE, WHICH I DO BELIEVE IN, what is that and where does it fit when one seeks to retell a thing from its beginning?

To narrate: from the Latin *narratus*, which is the plural of *narrare*, and stems from *gnarus*, or knowing, and relates to *gnoscere* or *noscere*, to know. So sayeth Webster's Ninth, which by that definition is itself a narrative compendium, for to know the meaning of words as its pages do is a form of narration.

And down from my shelf comes a *Glossary of Literary Terms* to say: "A narrative is a story, whether told in prose or verse, involving events, characters, and what the characters say and do." And then adds this, the best part: "It should be noted that there is an implicit narrative element even in many lyric poems."

One knows something, then, or comes to know something, and tells the story of coming to know it, or, in telling the story comes to know it. Shades upon shades, but none of them, let us note, associated with selling. No, for to know, to come to know, and to tell one's way into knowing—these are not of the order of merchandise but of gift.

Foot in America | DAVID SCHULTZ

SEPTEMBER 1946, 109 DEGREES. Pinek Zelner sitting in Benjamin Feldman's next-door apartment. He slid ten, spread fingers down his face.

"I b-boil like a chicken in your New Jersey summer—"

"So we can have you for dinner."

"You're very funny, Mr. Feldman."

"But you can't only wear underpants. And in front of my girls."

"Be serious, *Benjomin*. The whole building sees your wife's—"

"But her bathing suit is not underpants," Ben said, tapping irritatedly on his salesman's sewing machine catalog. "And she dresses tasteful."

"—winkly giblets—"

"My wife has a name—it's Minna—"

"—sticking out in the back yard where everybody can see."

"Anyway, people don't go visiting half-dressed like you."

Ben cocked his chin at somewhere below Pinek's chest. He hoped he had not spoken cruelly to this man wearing a patch where an eye had been, whose postwar white-metal teeth had largely turned black—for which he probably did not have replacement money—and who had ugly scars running from his forehead to his lips.

"This rubber burns," Pinek said, tugging on the waistband of his boxers. A concentration camp prisoner's tattoo of one letter and five numerals came into view on his forearm.

"Please, wear regular pants like other people," Ben said.

Pinek smiled and exhaled cigarette smoke. "My fly is locked up. Look." He touched the two diaper pins securing the front of his shorts. "See?"

Ben waved as if shooing flies and stood up. "That's enough about weather, your fly, and my wife's bathing suit—I'm bringing you your machine."

Ben trudged up four floors with the Singer sewing machine in his chubby arms and tapped on Pinek's door with his foot. Pinek appeared, carrying a chipped plate of sausage. This garlicky, fatty Polish food, Ben thought, had to be a reason why the man looked colorless and skeletal—older than thirty-four. There had been the war in Europe, hunger, and now this disgusting food. He did not expect to be invited inside and wasn't.

"My doctor told me not to shlep heavy stuff," he said, panting.

"Have some sausage," Pinek said, offering the dish. "It'll make you strong. It's made in America." He grinned.

"No thanks," Ben said, returning a grin. "Losing weight and getting stronger is a lost cause for me." His grin broadened.

"You brought the belt, bobbins, and a motor?" Pinek asked.

"I brought you an extra bulb, a spare belt, and half a dozen bobbins, as promised. I can't give away a two-hundred-dollar motor. Listen, this machine is a monster to carry."

"America, thief," Pinek muttered, and turned his face toward the kitchen, then back to Ben.

Ben's face was somber. "America is a thief? Okay, don't buy this!" He pivoted toward the stairway.

Pinek called to his back, "*Idiota*, c-come back."

Ben turned. "This is my country. When I came here to live with an old widow aunt in Brooklyn, no family and no friends, I washed sinks and toilets in office buildings."

"Okay, Mister America," Pinek said, grinning, "come inside."

It was Ben's first time in the flat. Three mismatched folding chairs hung with faded baby bibs stood around the kitchen table. The air smelled of rosewater and he remembered that Minna had used it for years in place of the rather expensive scents she used now. She once said to him, "Honey, when I'm using the perfumes I'd like to have, I think I'll smell even sweeter to you."

He placed the machine on the table. "Here's your Singer 122K—a winner."

Pinek tipped the machine. "I see 'EY' on here—made in Estonia."

"What do you mean, Estonia? EY is Scotland. Singer makes their best machines there."

"I was fooling. Calm down."

"It's amazing what you know despite the war."

"You think only Americans know things? Are you an Indian?"

"Of course not; my family came from Poland, like you."

"So how can you be an American?"

"What do you mean?"

"I mean that real Americans are Indians, the screwed-over American Indians."

"So?"

"Listen—my father built two sewing mills and hired three hundred Polaks, but I don't have—"

"You're a good tailor, stop complaining."

"God gives you teeth—does that mean you have food to eat?"

"I mean that you'll make money with this beauty," Ben said, stroking the Singer.

"You're promising me that? A *promise-promise*, like kids say?"

"For God's sake, Zelner, already you want to be Rothschild? You—"

"Look, people want to buy fancy children's clothes, but my big fingers can't sew the little buttons and lacy embroidery. How will I pay for Alvin's education if he wants to be professional? No—I want him to be professional—a lawyer or real estate man." He popped a chunk of sausage into his mouth and wiped the hand on the tablecloth.

Ben said, "You don't waste your money, so you'll do okay. Just give it some time."

"Oh yeah, time. How much time?"

"A reasonable amount."

"And after that I'll have a Mercedes-Benz with a convertible top. Like a rich American."

"Mercedes doesn't make convertibles."

Pinek stood up, stretched his arms out sideways and danced in a circle, mock crooning, "Everything is possible in America."

Ben pointed to the one photo on the wall. "Beautiful horse."

"Her name was Kawalerzysta. It's Polish for cavalryman."

"She was yours?"

"No, my little soldier brother Shimon. He was seventeen; the Polish army sent horses against German armor. He rode her 'til a tank killed them. They were telling us over the radio that the German tanks were cardboard. Stupid Polaks."

"I'm sorry," Ben said.

"Yeah. Okay, today is labor day, I got to do sewing."

Pinek reached up to the wall shelf next to the kitchen table and took down the bowl of diaper pins. He took a roll of money from it.

"Here. Write a receipt," he said.

"Why? I live next door to you."

"Isn't a receipt required insurance in America? Slide it under my door."

Minna spoke to Ben in bed that night. "Why did he call today Labor Day? Labor Day is over."

"The eye patch and scars are horrible," Ben said.

"Stop, Benny, we didn't do it to him. Anyway, he came out pretty good, thank God, even with the scars and the one eye." She kissed him.

"He says I'm making my health worse, selling the machines from my trunk," Ben said.

"You can slow down—"

"And then we'll go outside and eat grass."

"You know," Minna said, turning off the bed lamp, "he married a lady who's a smart wife and mother, so he should be fine."

"So with such a wife, what's wrong with him?"

"He's got war shock. It mixes up his thinking."

Morning had just broken when Pinek in undershorts carried the garbage downstairs to the garbage shed behind the building. A large carton imprinted with "Super 17 Inches" and "America Needs RCA" lay near the shed. American style advertising, he thought. But such a large screen would be kind to Anna's and his eyes—hers sapped by two nightly nursings and his strained from sewing for hours by a ten-watt light bulb. He carried the carton three blocks to his old car that was parked in the abandoned factory area that people said was roamed by dangerous tramps. He placed the box on the back seat and drove back to the building. He unscrewed the torn seats and carried them upstairs to the apartment, one at a time, leaving the carton as his driver's seat. Anna had agreed to remove the seats' stuffing—texture of stale crackers—and replace it with old newspapers he had scavenged in the building hallways.

He was eager to try the carton seat. It collapsed when he had only driven a few yards. Sunk low on it, he drove into a beer delivery truck. He managed to drive to the apartment, but one leg was painfully fractured. That same morning Ben drove him to an orthopedic clinic where they fitted him with a cast and crutches. The clinic manager permitted him to owe his fee for six months.

"This is the first time in America somebody isn't making me pay right away," Pinek said to Ben while they drove home. "Me, an immigrant yet."

"In America the thief, yet," Ben said.

That afternoon, six children in underpants were splashing each other with pails of cool water in the back yard. Pinek's ten-year-old son, Alvin, crept up behind fourteen-year-old Dora Bronstein, yanked off her bra, and ran off with it, whooping.

She gave chase and caught up to him. Her slap sent him into a bush of stinging nettles as he struggled to push his chubby body through a hedge. He managed to get onto his knees, but another slap sent him flat onto rough concrete. He stood up with bleeding face and knees.

"You whore, my father will knock the crap out of you!"

"Your father's a dumb Polack, walks around in undies, and everybody sees it," Dora shouted back.

Alvin ran upstairs to Pinek who was at work at the Singer. He burbled, "I only pulled her top a little."

Pinek saw in his son's face his father's anguish when a Polish Nazi collaborator slapped him. The man's companion had dropped the keys to Pinek's father's Horch convertible into a briefcase and had told his father: "Your keys will have a lot of Jew company in my briefcase."

Pinek stroked Alvin's face. Then he grabbed a crutch and hobbled down the building's rear stairs. Mrs. Kolbitz, who had sometimes babysat Alvin, was coming up the steps, carrying a large box and breathing hard.

She crooned her customary "Hello, mister, how's your wife and son?"

"We're fine," Pinek said. "Listen, my wife's massages can help your muscles and make you breathe better. She learned medical massaging in Poland."

Mrs. Kolbitz touched his crutch. "Massaging might help me more than the doctors. I'll think about it."

Entering the back yard, Pinek saw Dora Bronstein chatting with friends and hobbled toward her. Her wild kick struck his wounded leg. He slapped her with his free hand and she fell.

He raged, "That's for beating Alvin."

Dora's father obtained a court summons that afternoon. The examiner at the hearing, a man sporting an imperial mustache and silk jacket, cheerily greeted the defendants with "Hello, neighbors" from his table at the front of the room. But when he asked Pinek about striking Dora Bronstein and Pinek admitted to it, the man fined him two hundred and fifty dollars and warned him to unconditionally avoid the Bronsteins.

Pinek fumed, "Tell that girl with a woman's giblets to keep away from my son or I'll come for some better American justice."

The examiner paused a moment.

"Mr. Zelner, I'm excusing your intemperate words, but hitting that young girl is inexcusable. I'm still fining you the two hundred and fifty dollars."

"You're an ox," Pinek said.

"And you are risking contempt of court," the examiner snapped. "Watch yourself."

"Watch your stupidity," Pinek shouted.

"That's it," the examiner barked. "Bailiff, take him to room 107."

Pinek was escorted from the hearing room and Anna was told that she could wait for him. When Pinek was released into the hallway an hour later, she was waiting.

She clutched his sleeve. "*Idiota!* We're lucky he didn't do worse to you when you ran your mouth at him."

"'Intemperate' means what?"

"I don't know. Anyway, he was not so rough, except for the fine—two hundred and fifty dollars."

"I won't pay it."

"And you'll go to jail."

"*Anka*, they really screw you here, don't they?"

Delivery day came and Pinek walked to his newly acquired twelve-year-old car to deliver garments to customers. No neighbor acknowledged his hand greeting. That afternoon he went to buy lining material for women's suits. Exiting from the wholesaler's shop, he saw Mrs. Kolbitz straining to carry two large bags.

"Hello, Mrs. Kolbitz," he called, "Let me help."

"Child abuser! Don't come near me!"

Pinek stood silent for a moment. "That's not true."

She waved a fleshy fist. "You should be ashamed. Maybe you abuse your wife, too."

Pinek megaphoned to her with his hands. "Hey, that fifty pounds of gold around your neck can kill you, ridiculous witch!"

Pinek's concentration-camp headaches returned that afternoon. Mornings would become the only time of day he could concentrate on sewing.

Pinek was on his chore of food shopping. Standing in line at Katz's grocery, he heard neighbors talking about an old man named Kramer who lived in his building and who had been attacked and beaten. They said the attack had occurred in the abandoned lot behind the tailor shop and the luncheonette. Wanting to be alone and think about what he had heard, Pinek stopped at Meyer's Novelties and bought a musical doll for baby Lina and a gyroscopic top for Alvin. As he hobbled toward the bus stop, a dark-skinned man approached along the same sidewalk with something long in his hand. Pinek dropped one crutch and gripped the sharp old German jackknife he had owned since the end of the war. He held it with its point facing forward and waited. The man crossed the street and disappeared.

Pinek decided not to mention the incident to Anna.

When he handed her his gifts, she said, "You're more caring about the children now."

"I don't want people to call me 'child abuser' like Kolbitz did."

"I know, *Pineczku*," she said, circling him in her arms. "I know."

"I want to talk to the store owners about Kramer," he said.

"Don't. Everybody will think you're looking for more trouble."

"I want some respect."

"What you'll get, my clever husband, is more disrespect."

"Why are you so scared about what Jews, our own Jews, think of us?"

Running her hand gently over Lina's head, Anna said, "American Jews were not in the concentration camps. We get scared more."

"Maybe you do."

Anna sighed. "I'm finished," and sat down on the one sofa chair. She took a large jar off the end table and Pinek watched her rub ointment into her raw-chafed hands. He remembered Doctor Holo Kornfeld and their sleeping places on the same plank in the camp barrack. Holo was hanged for giving food to other prisoners. Before the hanging, German soldiers had made a horse drag him over gravel mixed with fragments of glass. Pinek's memory was mixed with the thought that Holo's compassion was where his youthful faith in God had gone and thus was not completely shattered.

He rubbed ointment into Anna's swollen ankles. "*Kocham Cię*," he said, having seldom said he loved her but feeling a need to say it now. "*Ankele*," he added. "I wonder if anybody from our camp is still alive and where." He sat down on the floor in front of her chair and laid his head in her lap.

"*Pineczku* dear," she said softly, "I loved you at first sight." In moments they were asleep.

As sunlight streamed into the bedroom in the morning, Pinek donned the khaki shorts he had received from war-refugee relief. These provided him enough ventilation to prevent his suffering from heat rash over his lower body. Struggling on his crutches, he rode the bus to his appointment with the police.

Detective James Fitzsimmons pointed him to a chair.

Pinek studied the white goatee that resembled his father's. He saw himself, seven years old, with his father at the Turkish bath in Łódź city. Outdoors after they had left the baths, his father, seeing him shaking with cold in that severe winter, bought him a wool sweater at a class shop on Lutomierska Street. Picturing his father adjusting the sweater to sit properly on him always stung his eyes.

"Mr. Zelner," Mr. Fitzsimmons said, "here are photographs of Mr. Kramer after the beating."

Pinek put on his glasses. "I saw worse," he said.

"During the war, I guess."

"Are there lots of attacks on Jews in America?"

"Some, not very many nowadays, I think."

"I will tell you something," Pinek said. "A woman in Łódź, my city, wanted to buy flour to bake Passover matzos. So she went to the market and waited until they closed to buy some that didn't get sold, if she was lucky. A Polish farmer offered her exactly the amount she needed for a few *zlotys*—a bargain. He filled a sack to the top and weighed it in front of her. At home she found the sack was filled with *świńskie gówno*. You understand Polish?"

The detective smiled. "I learned some Irish expressions from my grandma."

"'Pig shit.' He sold her pig shit."

Detective Fitzsimmons paused. "Anti-Semites desecrate synagogues and cemeteries, but they don't usually attack people physically," he said.

"You think every single thing gets known?"

"No, of course not. Anyway, Mr. Kramer only told us that the attack happened behind a couple of stores—but not which. There are seven stores on that street."

"I'll get you information," Pinek said.

"It could be dangerous. Very."

"How do you make soup?"

"Don't have the slightest idea—Mrs. Fitzsimmons does all the cooking."

"You peel onions. If the onions make you cry, you don't stop peeling. Then you cook them and get soup."

"Mr. Zelner, the attack on Mr. Kramer is police business."

"But maybe the police don't care about some beaten-up old Jew."

The detective caught the glasses that had started to slide down his nose.

"I'm not Jewish, Mr. Zelner, but my people—Irish immigrants—suffered discrimination in this country, so I asked to handle Mr. Kramer's hate case."

Pinek offered his pack of cigarettes and smiled.

"No, thank you, Mr. Zelner. If I had some witnesses I could get them to identify those animals."

"Like I said, I can try to get you witnesses."

"Like I said, you can get hurt."

"You know, chickens, even cooked ones, don't fly into your mouth."

The detective chuckled and stroked his goatee. "An apt saying, Mr. Zelner. Still, you could get hurt."

"Anyway, I live in the same building as Mr. Kramer so I can visit him easy. You police don't live in our underprivileged area."

"Well, if you learn something, please call me," the detective called as Pinek went toward the door, crutches thumping the wood floor.

Several hours later, as Pinek entered the cleaning store, Nathan Miller looked up from inspecting a sweater and pointed at the coat hanging on the rack beside him.

"How much is this mink worth to you?" he asked.

Pinek wondered, as he had many times, where his mother and sisters' prettier coats went after the Nazis had sent them to death.

"I would like some information," he said.

"About the coat?"

"No. My friend. Kramer says he was attacked behind your store," Pinek said, the spontaneous untruth appearing brilliant to him.

Miller stared at him with watery eyes. His head shook with tremor. "You got a permission paper from the court?"

"No, but—"

"End of discussion, mister."

"I need a court p-paper to just talk to you?"

"I don't know anything more. And I need a garbage barrel through my window again like I need . . ." he said, drawing a finger across his throat.

Pinek glanced at the street window with three tailor dummies standing inside it. He quickly raised his crutch and prodded one of them. The mannequin tottered and fell, taking another down with it.

"Bastard," Miller shouted, rushing toward the window. He lifted the fallen dummies, swearing, while Pinek went onto the street, lighting a Camel cigarette and examining his yellowed fingers. He felt no guilt over his untruth claiming friendship with Kramer, nor over knocking Miller's mannequins down. He hobbled into Kaufman's Luncheonette next door and ordered coffee at the counter. The cup Kaufman hurriedly set down in front of him looked as if it might land in his lap. He swept his hand to stop it, sending it sliding toward the sugar dispenser and onto the floor next to Kaufman's feet.

"I just want to ask you about Mr. Kramer, if—" Pinek said.

"Do me a favor and go," Kaufman said. "You're the guy who slapped the girl."

"That's settled."

"So you say. Her face is still swollen and she won't show herself at school."

"I said that's finished."

"You can just go. No charge for the coffee."

Pinek left. His experiences of the Jewish store owners abandoning other Jews left him infuriated but thinking that he might have achieved more by having been less direct with them.

When Pinek arrived home, Anna quickly served him his dinner, figuring he had gotten very hungry from all his visits downtown. He picked morosely at his plate of boiled chicken and potatoes. Anna sat near him and watched.

"I got nowhere with the store owners," he said. "Do you want to live here?"

"We pay the lowest rent in the building and we have neighbors who are nice— when they're not furious with you."

"The low-class big-mouths."

They heard Lina crying and went into the bedroom.

"She looks so red," he said, and shook a rattle near her face.

"Don't do that," Anna said, "you'll scare her."

Pinek put his face close to the baby's. "You're my *manivil.*"

"She's not ugly," Anna said. "She's beautiful."

"The devil doesn't hurt the children you call ugly."

"Pinek, Lina needs clothes and Alvin needs a winter coat," Anna said.

"I can't sew the little details on the clothes for Lina. People would buy baby clothes from us if I could do that work. I only can make the coat for Alvin."

"We can find the baby clothes at the shul bazaar. But when will you have time to make the coat for Alvin? You've got to finish that woman's coat on time."

"Don't I always finish on time?"

Anna realized that her remarks were unwarranted. "True, you do finish on time,

Pineczku. Maybe we can get Alvin's coat at the bazaar."

"Did we come through the camps so our children can wear somebody's rags?"

"But it won't always be this way," Anna said, stroking his hand. "You can learn to do whatever you want, even how to make baby clothes."

"Could you help me sew the little fancy details?"

"My hands could be too achy," Anna said, pushing a soiled diaper into a paper bag with other ones.

"I can't afford to hire anybody to help me."

"I could try to do the details, call it a second miracle."

"We're alive, that was our first one," Pinek replied.

In the morning, after her first nursing, Anna opened the apartment door to pick up the milk delivery. She found a sheet of paper with handwriting in Yiddish and brought it to Pinek who was working at the Singer.

He read aloud, "'Your hitting Dora Bronstein is ruining our shul's good name. You should not be members. Period.'"

Anna pressed a torn seam together in her nightgown's forearm. "That probably means we won't be welcome at the shul bazaar, period."

"The bastard didn't sign his name. Or her name."

"Where will we live if they make us to move?"

"They want me to dump Kramer."

"It would help."

"I don't want to do that, Anna."

"Okay, I'll give birth in the street."

At three a.m. Pinek awoke anxious, with tremulous hands. He watched Anna's face in the moonlight streaming in from the window and wondered if worry was eroding her Polish beauty, embittering her.

She opened her eyes. "What's wrong?"

"I only paid the girl back for hitting Alvin, that's all."

"It's not the first time you hit somebody."

"But never a female."

"No. But you smashed Hershel Fishman's eyeglasses on Sukkoth. You weren't even sure he stole your carfare money. Wasn't that your quick temper?"

"I got so m-mad because Alvin is just—"

"But what you do makes enemies and it woke you up."

"Shitty life," Pinek said.

"Shitty? You call our life that?"

The room went silent.

"I need to rest," Anna said. "I'm nursing the baby again in an hour."

She put her arm around her husband, whispered *Kocham Cię* in his ear, and he slept through the night.

Pinek awoke to the alarm clock ring he had set. While Anna continued to sleep with Lina in their bed, he boiled coffee in a saucepan and drank two cups. At a bit past nine he hobbled on his crutches downstairs to Kramer's apartment door and knocked softly. The door opened a crack. Over the latched chain he saw a wrinkled face with missing teeth and a bandaged cheek.

"Hello," he said through the narrow space. "I'm a neighbor—"

"Look, stop upsetting people—"

"I only need a minute."

A pause. Sol Kramer squinted. "Okay, come in—I need to sit."

Pinek entered the kitchen lit by a single dim bulb. A small gray parrot standing on its perch on the kitchen table said, "Hello stranger."

"Sit," Kramer said. "You're the first person to come here besides police. I have a son. He came after the attack, stayed an hour and went back on vacation. This parrot is different. He even talks to me a few times a day."

He offered the bird a seed and said, "I love you."

"That's awful treatment from a son," Pinek said. "Our prayer says, *Don't throw me out when I'm old and weak.*"

Kramer poured dark tea into a stained mug. Sipping the hot liquid made his swollen eye squint. Odors in the air, apart from the smell of wintergreen, reminded Pinek of squalid camp bodies. If he and Kramer were now in Łódź—as the city had been before the Germans—he would send a servant to help him. He leaned closer to him. "I need—we need—to do something about what they did to you because that bothers me more than my reputation around here."

"But we're strangers."

"Really such strangers?—haven't we been talking seriously? So maybe I can help us both."

"Your name again?" Kramer said, sipping his tea.

"Pinek. We have a boy and baby and my wife is expecting."

"Shouldn't you be with her instead of struggling with my problem?"

Pinek looked into Kramer's anxious face and laughed dryly. "Without a strategy a people falls."

"I don't know Talmud."

"It's a saying, not Talmud. The *Malakh Hamoves*, he's always waiting for us."

"I don't understand. Who is waiting?"

"The Angel of Death."

"Oh."

Pinek folded his hands on the table and Kramer saw the tattoo on Pinek's forearm.

"You were in a concentration camp?" he asked.

"Yah, but let's talk about the beating. What they did to you can't be ignored."

"Who won't ignore me?"

"Am I an invisible ghost, me, Pinek Zelner?"

"A ghost?" Kramer laughed.

"Look, I'm here with you, flesh and bones. And I'm not ignoring you, am I?"

"No, of course not," Kramer said, seemingly embarrassed.

"The police showed me photos of the beating—I-I saw your face."

"They hurt more than my face. Look."

Kramer slowly raised his shirt and twisted his body. Pinek saw the bright red and purple rib cage.

"Can you walk in the street with me?" he asked.

"I limp a little where they kicked me some hard ones, but my cane is a good leg." Kramer said, smiling. "When?"

"Now. I want us to see the tailor and the luncheonette man."

"I didn't mention them to the police. Why bother them?"

"That's okay. They need bothering."

At a table in the rear of Kaufman's luncheonette, Kramer and Pinek quietly drank tea. Kaufman approached, spreading cream over grill burns on his chubby arms.

"It's inhuman, what they did," he said to Kramer, seeming not to notice Pinek. "The marks on your face—"

Kramer chuckled, "I'm beautiful enough for God to take me."

"I'm here, too, Mr. Kaufman," Pinek said.

"You needed to drag a sick old man out of his house?" Kaufman retorted.

"I wanted to come," Kramer said, "because the police have no witness of the attack."

Kaufman turned to Pinek. "So you're some kind of good-deed-doer for Mr. Kramer, eh?"

"Well," Pinek said, "I came—"

"Yeah, to give us more trouble."

Pinek pushed his tea away. "Listen, d-d-damn it, I came because—"

"I know. Family members I never got to meet were murdered in Poland." He grasped Pinek and Sol Kramer's wrists. "Come with me."

He led them through the door behind them into an empty lot. Hibiscus and sunflowers were still in bloom on the cool, late summer evening.

"Look," he said, pointing to the brick walls flanking the door.

Pinek saw KILL JEWS painted on each wall. "When did it happen?" he asked.

"Before they saw Kramer to beat him," Kaufman said. He scanned the weed lot behind them, as if looking for someone lurking there. "I was home," he said, pointing up at the building's second floor windows. "Miller was playing *klaviash* with me and my missus. He was getting the best cards. We heard screaming and looked out the window. Two big *bullvans* were punching and kicking Kramer and hollering and whooping—awful sounds."

"Why didn't you call for help?" Pinek asked.

Kaufman said, "I wanted to run down here with a butcher knife, but Miller and my wife panicked. So we put away the cards, called the cops and talked till four a.m. Miller kept talking about those sounds."

"I know the sounds better than you," Pinek said. "Don't wash away what they wrote on the wall."

"I won't."

"And I want you and Kaufman to talk to the police."

A week later, at their 8:30 appointment with the police, Kaufman drove Miller and Pinek to attend the morning lineup. At 9:24, Miller and Kaufman left the viewing room and entered the hallway where Pinek sat waiting on a bench.

"Well?" he asked.

"Why do you want to get us killed, Zelner?" Kaufman said. "Why?"

"What did you tell the police?" Pinek asked.

"We picked the same two guys." Kaufman said "Okay?"

Miller's head was trembling. "One guy threw his shoe at the viewing window. That helped me pick him. Bastard screwed himself."

Pinek swung a crutch toward the ceiling and held it like a flag. "What you did will help Kramer."

Kaufman grimaced. "Yeah, the cops said they will send us a letter about what'll happen to those guys," he said doubtfully. He sat down on the bench and rubbed his calf. "Doctor called it 'aggravated neuralgia' from standing a lot in my store."

"Kaufman, you did great," Pinek said, "So smile".

"Not so fast. We only win if they lock those guys away so they can't come after us."

"Don't worry about them," Pinek said to calm Kaufman's anxiety.

Kaufman and Miller walked toward opposite exits. Pinek sat listening to their retreating, diverging footsteps. He thought of the divergences from the business owner's life he had expected to lead, until the Germans invaded; and the divergence, such as his and Anna's being spared from death was perhaps a miracle, as was perhaps a chance to now enjoy and cultivate their lives in a new place, as had been gifted to the Jews in the Five Books.

Entering the apartment after the ride home from the police station, Pinek found Anna nursing Lina at the kitchen table and nibbling on bits of sausage.

"Both of them picked the same two bastards," he said.

"Meaning what?" Anna asked.

"Meaning that since Miller and Kaufman saw the same guys beating Kramer, those guys will get tried and put away. I hope."

Anna said, "Here, Minna brought us these. And there's a card."

She drew some garments from a shopping bag and spread them on the empty table. Mixed with the old baby clothes were some new-looking boys' and men's shirts and a woman's silk blouse.

Pinek read the card aloud, "'Best wishes from Minna and Ben.'"

Anna pinched his thigh. "You see? We have friends. Maybe we won't need to buy from the flea market."

"Still, we didn't get a membership renewal from the shul," Pinek retorted.

He sat down and stared at a pile of unpaid letters on the table.

"Bills," he said.

"Only two—the rest are just advertisements you can throw away."

Pinek, Alvin, and Anna carrying Lina arrived to see Mr. Sachs, the shul president. Anna asked Alvin to sit in the outer office and wait.

Mr. Sachs, stout with sweaty circles under his arms, stood up behind his desk.

He pointed to two chairs with his cigar.

He said, "It's hot, how are you?"

"Cold," Pinek said.

Mr. Sachs laughed. "It's the air-conditioning."

"That's something new to me," Pinek said.

"Really? You don't know air-conditioning? Well, in Europe maybe . . . okay. Mr. Zelner . . . Pinek . . . , I received various telephone calls. People told me you mistreated—actually beat up—one of our child members and should not be a member of this shul, their shul."

"I didn't come to b-beg," Pinek said, rising from his chair. "Maybe I lost my head with the girl. But a Jew needs a shul for prayers, for a burial plot, a bar mitzvah, friends for wives and children, someplace to—"

"Look at this," Mr. Sachs said, taking a typed sheet of paper from his desk drawer and turning it toward Pinek. Pinek's name was printed in capitals.

"Do you understand this?" Mr. Sachs asked.

Pinek's mind was seized by the memory of his father being dragged off by armed Polish guards.

"It's about the girl?" he asked.

"It's the hearing examiner's judgment. Dora Bronstein's father gave me this copy. Mr. Kaufman and Mr. Miller phoned and told me you tried to get justice for Mr. Kramer. Mr. Miller sounded worried about the danger of identifying the criminals, but as the French say, you can't make an omelet without cracking eggs." He chuckled. "Listen. My job is to tell you that our board appreciates what you did for one of its frail, older members who's alone in the world."

He removed a handful of envelopes from his desk drawer and held them toward Pinek. "I also received these six letters of complaint. It comes down to this: it would be more comfortable for you and your family if you attended a different shul. The synagogues are all looking for members."

"Who sent the letters?" Pinek asked.

"I can't tell you that."

"Well, I don't talk to more than three people—neighbors—besides Kaufman and Miller."

Mr. Sachs had turned to raise the cooling control. He turned back to address Pinek: "Garden Street Synagogue offers similar activities to ours and lots of refugees like you are members there."

"What do you mean 'like you'?" Pinek said. "I'm not running. No more running. I live here. An immigrant tailor and his family. We want to take the citizenship class. I may start using Paul for my name instead of Pinek."

"That's wonderful. But you might feel more at home with the Garden Street people."

"I can feel at home with lots of people."

Mr. Sachs' chair squealed as he stood up. He pulled a cigar from his pocket and lit it with the ivory lighter on his desk.

"You're making things harder, Mr. Zelner. The Garden Street shul will give you memberships without any trouble."

"You're not calling me my first name? No more American style?"

"I understand why you can be upset."

The room was silent. Pinek started walking to the door.

"Don't go, stay with me," Anna called to him.

He returned and stood by her chair.

Anna said, "Mr. Sachs, you're still living with your refugee grandma who came from Europe like we did?"

"What do you mean?"

"Why should we go to other refugees? This is our shul and it's in America, isn't it? Where all people are equal?"

Mr. Sachs puffed his cigar with an unsteady hand and exhaled a cloud of smoke. "I've got no time to argue with you people," he said.

Pinek approached the desk and shook his finger in Mr. Sachs' face. "You, mister p-p-president of this shul, you can't forgive somebody who went crazy one time? You shouldn't have this job—you're a f-fucking f-fake—-"

Mr. Sachs grabbed Pinek's shirt. "You can't talk to me like that. I'll—" He pulled the shirt and part of the button strip came away in his fist.

Pinek felt the chill of air-conditioning where his shirt had opened.

Anna leaped from her seat.

While she restrained Mr. Sachs' hand from reaching Pinek again, Pinek slapped him, making his glasses fall onto the desk and blood run from his nose onto the desk and his upper lip.

"I'm calling the police," Sachs rasped.

Anna grasped Pinek's arm. She said, "Come on," to him and both quickly went out the door. Arriving at the secretary's desk, she gestured to Alvin.

"Mamma," Alvin said, "I heard . . . why did daddy fight the man?"

"No fight," Anna said. "They just were arguing."

"About what, mamma?"

"Stop, you two," Pinek said. "Alvin, listen, we have an understanding with the man in there. Sometimes understandings need some loud words."

The secretary raised her hand. "Oh, Mr. Sachs buzzed. He wants you to wait."

Pinek leaned toward Anna. "Maybe he's calling the police?" he whispered.

Anna snapped, "Shh. Be patient."

The intercom buzzed. The secretary listened to Mr. Sachs' voice, looked up and held out a sheet of paper.

"Mr. Sachs says to please fill this out and return it with the membership payment."

"He should have offered it before," Pinek said.

At the elevator, he put his arm around Anna and his other hand cupped Lina's head.

"How do you feel?" Anna asked.

"Can they arrest me?"

"He gave us our memberships, didn't he?"

"I could have hit him real good."

Anna pinched his ear. "Sh. Look, *Pineczku*, Lina's smiling."

"Nice," he said. "And I want to talk to Kramer's son."

Variations on a Beginning | M. ALLEN CUNNINGHAM

[8]

IN A SIXTH-CENTURY COURTYARD in North Africa a man hears a disembodied child's voice imploring him to take up the scriptures and read. Obeying, the man's eyes fall upon some words of Saint Paul and immediately "the light of confidence" floods his heart. He hurries inside his house to tell his mother he's been saved. This is Saint Augustine's moment of conversion as he himself describes it. In a single profound instant he awakens to his place in a larger story as told by Paul. His bright surge of spiritual "confidence" is the form of knowing peculiar to narrative. He has awakened to narrative's power—to narrative as a way of recognizing where one belongs, where one is rooted, narrative as a voice whose sole interest is discovery, coming to know, narrative as voice, which one may willingly follow.

Why I Didn't Go to the Firehouse | SOPHFRONIA SCOTT

THE FIREHOUSE IS THE SANDY HOOK VOLUNTEER Fire and Rescue station and it serves my neighborhood here in Newtown, Connecticut. Yes, that Sandy Hook. And yes to the question that I tend to get next: my son Tain did go to school at Sandy Hook Elementary and he was present in his third grade classroom on the morning of December 14, 2012 when a gunman entered the school and took the lives of twenty-six adults and children including one of Tain's dearest friends, a first-grader named Ben.

The firehouse is just down the road, perhaps only a few hundred yards from the location of the school. Dickenson Drive is the name of the street and that's appropriate because it is more like a long driveway than a road, leading only to the small parking lot in front of the school. The firehouse is constructed of red brick and the doors of the bays housing the fire trucks are wide and white. Each year after Thanksgiving my family and I visit the firehouse and choose a tall, bushy evergreen from the inventory of Christmas trees the firemen sell as a fundraiser. We pay more than if we shopped elsewhere because we want to support this essential but all-volunteer service. The only other time I'd been in the firehouse was probably for a field trip when Tain was in preschool.

Not long after the news of the shootings broke the *New York Times* published a story that reported:

> Survivors gathered at the Sandy Hook Volunteer Fire and Rescue station house, just down the street. Parents heard—on the radio, or on television, or via text messages or calls from an automated emergency service phone tree—and came running.

I didn't.

I didn't come running.

I could have. The school is not far from my home and that morning I was even closer, at a nearby auto repair shop. But instead of driving out of the shop's parking lot, turning right onto Berkshire Road and speeding my way to Tain's school I turned left and went home. Why? And I think "Why?" is the more polite question. I get asked about this a lot, from family, friends, strangers. They ask, "What did you do when you found out?" I tell them I went home. Then there's a look on the face in front of me—blank like a sheet of new paper—and when I see that look it seems to me the question they really want to ask is, "How could you do that?" Even if they don't ask it outright, I know the question is there.

Different people handle things differently—we all know that, right? But when I see that look I know the person is running an emotional inventory that could place me somewhere from being a monk to a monster. The space within that range is broad but I think it's the extremes that fascinate the most. On the one end, to not go racing to the firehouse might seem to them faithful and stoic—picture me meditating in front of the Buddha I keep in my office at home—or on the other end, the reaction could seem cold and unfeeling, more nihilistic or existential, I suppose. What kind of mother are you? In that realm I'm a few wire hangers shy of Joan Crawford in *Mommie Dearest*. But no matter where I fall in someone's spectrum I can see why my response or non-reaction would be confusing, curious, challenging to my listener. Can I say it feels the same for me? It's so hard to explain.

Tell me you would have gone. Tell me how if it had been your son in that school and you would have raced right over there like all those parents on television. I will nod and perhaps even mumble something like, "Yes, well . . ." and not finish the sentence. Because your saying that won't get us any closer to the answer to your question. Or maybe that's the point. It's not really about what I did or didn't do. It's about you putting yourself in the picture. People constantly use that phrase, "I can't imagine . . ." and yet I find they do a wonderful job of doing just that. Even if they don't vocalize it I know they are playing out the possibilities.

But their calculations wouldn't include the variable of time. Specifically I mean everything I thought and did in the days, months, and years leading up to that morning. My response after hearing the news wasn't the reaction of a moment. The decisions I made in those early minutes were actually years in the making and informed by seemingly unconnected events. How do you talk about that in the course of a casual conversation?

The repetition of the question, however, tells me something or someone wants an answer. It may even be something deep within myself demanding accountability or acknowledgment. I won't know until I begin so I will attempt a response but I'm wary—the words I lay out here may only be breadcrumbs that get devoured by greedy ravens—gone that quickly. Or they may stay and pave a path or even a bridge to something more. I have no idea what will happen but I sense this is important and worth the risk. I will try. I'm going to revisit that morning as best I can, with a few prompts such as emails and texts aiding my memory but really, I'm not dependent on them. Such moments are as simple, fierce, and bracing as a cold clear winter day. There's not much you can do to smudge it up. There is only what is.

This essay is about a window of time, a space of approximately two hours, in which I didn't know if my son was safe.

Let's start with the morning or rather the glow of the morning—pale yellow December light, painted on by a well-worn brush. I had watched that glow develop from the early hours because at the time I was a substitute school bus driver, reporting for work often before 5:30 a.m. with Tain in tow. The dispatcher would hand me a route for a driver who'd called in sick and Tain would ride the bus with me, picking up and delivering first the high school and middle school students, then the intermediate school children. Then, if I wasn't driving a Sandy Hook route, I'd use my break to find a bus that was heading to his elementary school and put him on it before I went on to one of the other three K-5 schools in the Newtown district. I didn't drive to Sandy Hook that morning.

After 9 a.m. I was done, and I remember feeling that deep-breath kind of relaxation of work being done for the moment, of having my time be my own again for a little while. I left the bus terminal in my minivan, on my way to Tain's school. Why? I wanted to take a check into the office to refill Tain's lunch money card, which was how the children paid for their meals in the cafeteria. I could have mailed this in or done it online, but since my family was still new to Sandy Hook School (Tain had gone to a private school the previous three years) I liked taking such opportunities to visit in person—it was my way of getting more familiar with the principal, Dawn Hochsprung, and the rest of the office staff. I also wanted them to know me. Whenever I went in it seemed Dawn would come right out of her office to see who was there. She'd smile and ask about Tain. She was one of the reasons my husband Darryl and I agreed to make the switch to send Tain to Sandy Hook after Tain expressed an interest in going to school with his friends, including Ben and Nate, Ben's older brother. When we first visited the school I liked how she walked down the hall with Tain, listening carefully to his questions and making him feel as though it were already his school.

So I was on my way there when I remembered the cigarette lighter in the van wasn't working. Darryl had asked me to have it looked at because the next day he had to drive the van to some out-of-town event for the school where he taught 7th and 8th grade band. He needed the GPS, which has to be plugged in to the cigarette lighter. I didn't know how long a fix would take and I was due back to the bus terminal in the afternoon, so I decided to stop at the auto repair shop before going to the school.

I think about that particular decision a lot. I still remember the way the thought seemed to float in and settle upon me like a warm blanket—that soft and that obvious. My daddy used to have a saying, "My mind came to me . . ." whenever he remembered a forgotten detail or a thought occurred to him. This felt like that. My mind came to me and told me to get the van fixed first. I know—and for a long time I didn't tell this to anyone—if I had gone to Tain's school first I would have been there when the shootings happened. Maybe a few minutes before, maybe a few minutes after. Maybe I would have been in the office or the parking lot walking to the door.

At the auto shop a woman I knew from my church, Sherry, was in the waiting room. I sat with her and chatted. I remember while she waited for her car she was writing thank-you notes to parishioners who had pledged during the church's recent stewardship campaign. How long were we sitting there? Not long, maybe ten or fifteen minutes. A woman walked in with a confused look clouding her face. She pointed outside to the air behind her and said she'd gone to the high school (located across the street from the shop) to pick up her daughter for a dentist appointment but couldn't get in. Not even onto the grounds.

Then we heard the sound of sirens slashing cleanly through the cold winter air. Police cars sped past the auto shop.

They weren't stopping at the high school.

All at once it seemed our cellphones were buzzing, Sherry's, mine, and the woman's, with automated emails, texts, and voicemail messages from the Newtown School District. It said all of the schools were in a lockdown position with no one allowed in or out of the buildings because of a shooting at one of the schools. The messages didn't say which school. I remember the first breaking news report flashed on the screen of the television in the waiting room. Reports of a teacher shot in the foot. I remember thinking how absurd the story sounded. Once upon a time I had been a journalist so I was too familiar with the ridiculous nature of breaking news—how reporters can spew unconfirmed facts to fill the airspace that had been wrestled away from regularly scheduled programming. Sherry grew pale and I wanted to turn off the television.

Instead, I called the school bus depot—I figured the radio system there had access to the same emergency channels used by the police and ambulances. They would know something real. My supervisor answered the phone:

"Okay, Sophfronia, stay calm," he said. "The shooting is at Sandy Hook."

I said okay, then thanked him and hung up.

After that I was feeling my way through an unknown forest. Already I sought markers, trail blazes, anything that seemed familiar. I asked the shop owner for my van and I went outside to wait for it. Sherry has small children of her own in one of the other elementary schools. Her last words to me before I left the garage: "I'm sorry."

My phone was still in my hand and I stood in the parking lot looking down the road in the direction of the school. In my mind I was already halfway there. I'm supposed to be doing something. I'm supposed to be doing something. I wasn't sure what that something was. I had the odd feeling that I was trying to remember something, like I was trying to push through a thicket of brambles to reach a clearing where I could see and think. But despite this I was clear on the one thing I couldn't and could never seem to do in times of trial—I couldn't pray. I remarked on this to my pastor once and she had said, "That's when you have other people pray for you."

I opened the contacts app on my phone and found Pastor Kathie's number. The photo illustrating her file in my phone is of her, Tain and me on the day she baptized the both of us the year before. Tain is wearing a navy blue cardigan over his shirt and striped tie and he's holding a gift from his Sunday school class: a cross decorated with seashells. I touched the "Call" symbol next to Pastor Kathie's number. When I told her what was going on she asked in that calm, measured way of hers what I was going to do.

"I'm going over there," I said.

She gently pointed out that I wouldn't be able to do anything there. Her son Miles, an EMT first responder, was already on the scene; she reminded me of how small the roads are in that part of Sandy Hook, how they were most likely already congested, and we had to give the authorities the time and space to get a handle on whatever was going on. My stomach dropped. This could be worse than anyone expected.

"Okay." I may have even said "You're right," but I'm not sure because at that moment it didn't matter. I knew what I was going to do. She didn't say directly "Don't go," but it was like she had called me back to my right mind and I remembered. I remembered what it was I was supposed to do and I acted, but not out of what it may seem in this part of my account. I know this looks like an obvious answer for you: I didn't go to the firehouse because my pastor suggested against it. Seems simple enough. But her suggesting to me not to go and my listening to her is like saying I went skydiving and I jumped from the airplane because the guy strapped to my back said I had to—a choice but not really a choice.

To say this would discount the thought and preparation, conscious and un-conscious, poured into the foundation that one hopes will hold when a moment of crisis arrives. I've never been skydiving but I know in the training you learn how to pull your own ripcord, monitor altitude, and how to position your body so the fall is stable. But all the training in the world wouldn't account for the "screw you" variable that can show itself at any time and obliterate all that has come before it. This variable feeds on drama, fear, excess energy. It rises in the heat of the moment and whether you're skydiving or being presented with any kind of unwanted option you could easily say, even if it's not in your personality to do so, "Screw this."

Screw that, I'm not jumping.

Screw you, my child is in there. I'm going.

It would have been easy to react that way. I felt the pull of emotion and I could have given in to its undertow and told Pastor Kathie in one moment I wouldn't go to the school while doing just that in the next. But as I said, Pastor Kathie called me back to my right mind. I began to act—not out of obedience or even common sense—I began to act intentionally out of a promise I'd made to Tain and myself in the months before he was born.

Right when I arrived home Darryl called. The principal of the middle school where he teaches, about twenty minutes away, had come into Darryl's classroom, told him the news and said he could go home. He was on his way. I called my oldest brother, Vassie. We said a prayer together and stayed in touch throughout the morning. I turned on the television and heard the reporters spewing casualty numbers than seemed to change every few minutes. I turned it off again. I sat at my computer and sent e-mails to three friends chosen specifically because I trust their spirituality—

> There's been some sort of shooting at Tain's school. I'm calm but worried, scared. The place is surrounded by troopers and ambulance people. Roads are packed. Waiting here at home for news. Please, please send prayers. I know Tain must be fine and all will be well.

The words "worried" and "scared" weren't accurate but I think I included them because it's what's expected. I wasn't in a state of worry or fear—I was in a void. No, it's more than that. It was like I was in a void and the void was in me. I was holding this space of waiting and the holding of this space was the fulfillment of my promise to Tain.

How can I explain this?

I will tell you another story of waiting on another December morning, nine years before this one. I was pregnant then and, to me, miraculously so. I'd had a miscarriage a couple of years earlier and when Darryl and I couldn't conceive again we went through tests and discovered my uterus was scarred shut, a result of the treatment following the miscarriage.

My gynecologist referred us to an infertility specialist, Dr. K., on the west side of Manhattan. He performed surgery to remove the scar tissue. After a few weeks of healing I was supposed to start taking hormones and undergo more infertility treatment, scheduled to begin after I'd had a period. Only my period never came. We discovered I was already pregnant.

I loved that time of walking newly pregnant through New York City as the days were getting colder. I liked knowing I harbored my own bit of heat, a tiny ball of sunshine growing within me and waiting to warm its own universe. I lived in a realm of possibility and I remember being acutely conscious of it, of soaking up life and magic all around me—savoring the sugar of a Krispy Kreme donut melting in my mouth, my steps touching down on pavement that seemed gentle beneath my feet. I walked down Columbus Avenue and I saw a dual face, my own mingled with some aura of my unborn child, reflected to me in the smiling faces of strangers who couldn't possibly know I was pregnant. But in that strange law of nature, life attracts life, recognizes itself and feeds there. Every face seemed like a harbinger of grace, of the potential held by the being growing inside me. I felt a strong sense of the whole experience being a gift and I was grateful. I loved being in that golden bubble. It felt like where I was supposed to be. It felt like home.

Then suddenly—blood.

A Saturday morning, early December, with the first snowstorm of the season whipping a bitter wind past the windows of our sixth-floor apartment. I'd gone to the bathroom and found my underwear wet and heavy with thick red clots. The world shrank—shrank so fast the speed burned my eyes. What was so open and available to me the day before became in an instant only the four walls of that space and the bathroom door closed behind me.

I couldn't figure out what would come next. I didn't dare stand for fear of what

I might see in the water underneath me. Yet I wanted to get out of the stained underwear already dripping on the black and white tiles. At some point I know I reached for a towel hanging from the bar across from me. At some point I called out for Darryl to help me. But for the longest time I did nothing. The four walls were shrinking further into a hard dark knot and there was no room in there for Darryl, no room for me to even stand and take a step into the moment where I had to accept something was wrong and I had to move into the murkiness of what that meant and what I had to do.

I remember standing in the kitchen calling Dr. K with Darryl sitting on a stool and staring at a cold cup of coffee on the counter in front of him.

"What did the discharge look like?" the doctor asked.

The question made me recall gradations of color—pinks and magentas—apart from the stark red that initially shocked my eyes.

"Is it still happening?"

"Yes."

"I'll be in the office tomorrow morning. We'll do an ultrasound and we'll have a look."

Tomorrow?

Why didn't I argue with him? Why didn't I insist he see me that day? Because I knew Dr. K. I knew him well enough to know he didn't humor you or give false hope. He was more likely to say, "This is what we'll do" or "I want to have a look first and we'll see." His poker-faced way didn't make for a warm bedside manner but I never minded before. In fact I had pitied him because it seemed to me he needed to be that way from years of experience with frenzied, baby-yearning Manhattan women. But as I listened to him on the phone I realized his demeanor was for mornings just like this one. If he thought something could be done he would have told me to go to the hospital. I was losing the pregnancy and probably had to wait for the miscarriage to finish.

And then—darkness. There's the phrase from Psalm 23 about walking through the valley of the shadow of death but that morning it felt more like a tube—a dark but translucent tube. I could see the world going on around me and the tube was close enough that someone could walk next to me without realizing I was in it. But I knew I was in it, a tight place of sadness, unable to see to the other end. Inside the tube I tried to maintain the form and potential of a child I wouldn't get to know. I wanted this because I wanted something more to mourn than the flow draining from between my legs and because the sense of joy I'd had was once so tangible.

Outside the tube the rest of the world moved on. Darryl and I were supposed to attend a wedding that day. I'd been looking forward to it because when my friend Katherine had first introduced Mike to us I somehow sensed he would be the guy she married. I was thrilled when they got engaged and excited for the wedding. But that morning I felt heavy with grief, like all my cells were filled with it, bursting with it. I sat on the couch and hoped for a phone call saying the weather had forced Katherine and Mike to postpone. However, it wasn't the shut-down-the-city kind of snowstorm. The slushy streets were clogged with slow-moving traffic but you could still walk around, and the trains were running. When it became obvious there'd be no cancellation and Darryl asked if we were still going, I didn't have it in me to say no.

I put on a tan suit—pants and a long jacket to camouflage my bloated waist-line—and I went. There are photos of me from that day and looking at them now I can see I was pale. My smile was a game one. I was managing, just hanging on, but faking it all the same. All I wanted to do was go home and go to bed. The wedding and reception took place at a facility in Chelsea right on the Hudson River. If I didn't have the pictures to remind me I was there I might not have remembered much else. I remember the wall of windows showcasing the snow swirling outside on the pier. I remember the bride's broad smile. I remember how the whole space, vibrant with music and voices, was too loud for me to think about how to let go of all the promise my baby-to-be had contained.

The next day at the doctor's office I lay there in the dark, Darryl next to me while Dr. K moved the sensor around within me. I tried to make sense of the fuzzy, wavy lines, but then I saw it: an amazing, pulsating drop of light, insistent and strong.

"There's your baby," the doctor said. "Normal, six-week growth; heart beating and everything."

Darryl asked some questions and Dr. K. answered them—I think he used the words "implantation bleeding" and "normal" but I wasn't listening. I just kept staring at the image on the screen. I was talking to it, saying to it in my heart where only he and I could hear,

I will never give up on you again.

I had walked through that darkness when I didn't have to; and even worse, I'd unwittingly taken my child with me when I did it. The notion damn near overwhelmed me. I'd chosen to believe in death instead of life, had allowed fear to hijack my hope. I focused on the image of my unborn child and promised him I wouldn't do it again. I realized in that moment I must always believe in this little being's life. I had to believe it for both of us. And I still do. That doesn't mean I exist with a Pollyanna kind of hope, acting like Tain, now gloriously present in the world, will never know illness or will never die—because this will happen to all of us. But I do choose to make a simple choice to believe in the greater possibility of life over death, to believe first that life will find a way. It means that as long as Tain's life is a fact, I will live and breathe the joy of it until I know for certain that it's time for me to do otherwise. I hope I will never know such a time, as the grieving Sandy Hook mothers whose children didn't come home now do. However I will not, through fear and worrying, walk myself through the dark valley before I come to it.

So I live out this promise. On any given day it might look like a constant letting go, of watching my son leap from the nest in ways large and small and believing only in his growing ability to fly. My friend Cornelia recently told me it's like I am holding a space for Tain, a space of infinite possibility made all the more powerful because it is his mother who holds it for him. That sounds right to me.

Your question now may be: couldn't I have done that, hold such a space, while waiting at the firehouse with the other parents? Group energy is a powerful thing. History has shown us that being in the presence of a crowd can make people act out of character. They fold into the groupthink mentality. If I had gone to the firehouse and walked into that highly emotional brew I probably would have, out of instinct and compassion, mirrored back the concern in the faces of the people around me. And there would be no way to do that without eventually feeling the fear and concern myself. I know how easy it would have been, surrounded by sirens and cameras and weeping, to fret that Tain was injured or dead. I could have lived his death a thousand times in the span of those few hours.

I didn't.

At 11:05 a.m., I received the text from my friend Fran.

Tain is OK.

I typed back fast, while at the same time wanting to collapse to my knees.

How do you know??

I just saw him with his class.

Thank you!!!!! And Nate and Ben?

I can't find Ben.

Within a few minutes another friend was calling with Tain on the phone. "Hey bud!" I said. "How are you doing?" I wanted to send him light through my voice, light that would warm him and help him feel a touch of normal in the maelstrom surrounding him.

"Good!"

He said it like he always does, so that the word is almost two syllables with the second syllable toning up like a bounced ball.

I listened for signs of tremors or tears in his voice but I heard none. The one word "good" sounded so like him that I didn't question him about what was happening. I remember I told him Papa was on his way to bring him home.

That night I would have to tell Tain his friend Ben had died. That night and in the weeks and months to come I would have to hold the space for him. I continue to hold it so Tain can see there is room, always room, even when death has entered, for life—for what comes next, for what we need to do to comfort Fran, a mother who can no longer hold such a space for her lost son.

Think of the wingspan required to hold such a space. Think of how the space must be as broad and deep as the path you hope is open to any child of the world. Think of what such a task asks of your body and being and what it means to hold onto a promise that was never spoken aloud. Now you have your answer and so do I. All this is why I didn't go to the firehouse.

Pantoum for the End of the World | PEPPER TRAIL

Let's not talk about the end of the world today
Sitting here in the sun, with our cookies and our tea
The frogs singing around their little pond
The sky open again, after long closed weeks

We are sitting in the sun, with our cookies and our tea
The almond tree is hidden in a haze of bloom
After long closed weeks, the sky has opened again
But you lean close and ask "How bad will it be?"

The almond tree is hidden in a haze of bloom
I would escape into that haze of pink and green
But you lean close and ask "How bad will it be?"
And everyone falls silent, hungry for the worst

I would escape into spring's confusion
Join the chorus of the frogs and of the birds
But everyone is silent, hungry for the worst
So I must darken the day with prophecy

I would join the chorus of the frogs and of the birds
Slip through this net I wove myself
Yet I must darken the day with prophecy
Return again to my grim imaginings

Caught in this net I wove myself
I carry into the garden the glaciers, gone
Return again to my grim imaginings
Inhale: the waters rise; exhale: drought

I carry into the garden the glaciers, gone
Nods and murmurs greet the news
Inhale: the waters rise; exhale: drought
And still, you wait for more, and worse

Your nods and murmurs greet the news
I wonder, did swallows grace the eaves of Troy?
Did Cassandra watch them as she waited for the flames?
How insatiable we are, for hope and fear

Did swallows grace the eaves of Troy?
How marvelous, to be so ignorant and free
How insatiable we are, for hope and fear
Let's not talk about the end of the world today

Bud Light in an Idaho diner during another shooting

| DYLAN D. DEBELIS

I am writing this on a placemat in a diner
somewhere after Boise. With a crayon
I am tracing the map of the United States. I am
a radio losing its rhythm between time zones.

For all our talk of symmetry
the heart always shuts down one ventricle at a time.
Frostbitten toes fall off one by one until the knee is sawn off.
Young Adult novels talk about Chinese railroad labor
placing chopsticks between their teeth during amputation.

We gnaw our cheeks again tonight
and the rivulets of our blood fill the cracks between the Adirondacks
    and the Rockies
until the storm plains flood with dogwoods blooming
crimson topography. I wonder, from that far off
did your breath witness the factory blowout
by shivering slightly, enough for you to rise from your mattress
and ease the window closed, enough to stare out at the Louisiana live oak
    just for a moment
and wonder how far down the roots reach.

Or did your brain think better of stirring, instead
turning into your pillow
and waking a few hours later to the sounds of meadowlarks ushering in a
    late February dawn.

For my part, I kept driving

until the snow melted to reveal the carcasses
of creatures who went missing months ago.

Pincushion | LESLIE MILLS

I'm so annoyed.
United Health Care called twice,
once to remind me to have my eyes checked,
again to ask if I had any questions.
Yes, I have a question——why must you call me?
Has news of my imminent dementia
been entered prematurely
into your database?

It's true, I'm a wilting blossom –
just the thought of vacuuming does me in.
I'm overwhelmed by reading material,
technology continues to go over my head,
at doctor visits I turn into a disobedient child.
I even whimper sometimes when alone,
feeling sorry for poor little me.
But I am still capable
of scheduling an appointment
without assistance.

Meanwhile, in Missouri people lose homes,
lives, possessions as rivers overflow.
Houses burn in California,
are swallowed in mud, slide off cliffs.
Syrian and Somali refugees flee,
drown in the ocean, trudge across entire nations
seeking a better life for their children.

Everywhere, human beings are shot, exploded, starved,
oppressed, imprisoned, raped, mutilated,
tortured, arrested, discriminated against.
And here I sit, on my comfy sofa of entitlement,
whining about pinpricks caused by minute arrows
shot from tiny bows.
Saint Sebastian of the Petty Sorrows,
that's me.

Found, October 18, 1848 | FREDERICK W. BASSETT

They found me Sunday last
near Clinton Road
about five miles from Macon,
my fiddle flung by the wayside.
The Georgia Journal and Messenger
said I was well dressed
in a light purple frock coat
and pantaloons-blue Kentucky jeans
with extra fiddle strings in my pocket
but no papers on me.

The coroner held an inquest over me
but couldn't develop a clue about who I was.
Now don't get it in your head
that he was digging for the name
that the big house gave me
like my mama didn't have a tongue.
What he meant was he didn't know where
to send word: No need to post a reward.
They found your Negro dead,
shot in the head more than a week ago.

Variations on a Beginning | M. ALLEN CUNNINGHAM

[9]

I'VE LONG LOVED THE BIBLICAL STORY of Samuel, which is about hearing a voice, about listening and coming to know.

Samuel was lying down in the temple of the Lord, where the ark of God was. Then the Lord called "Samuel! Samuel!" and he said, "Here I am!" and ran to Eli, and said, "Here I am, for you called me." But Eli said, "I did not call, my son; lie down again." So he went and lay down. The Lord called again, "Samuel!" Samuel got up and went to Eli and said, "Here I am, for you called me." But Eli said, "I did not call, my son; lie down again."

Now Samuel did not yet know the Lord, and the word of the Lord had not yet been revealed to him. The Lord called Samuel again, a third time. And he got up and went to Eli and said, "Here I am, for you called me." Then Eli perceived that the Lord was calling the boy. Therefore Eli said to Samuel, "Go, lie down; and if he calls you, you shall say, 'Speak, Lord, for your servant is listening.'" So Samuel went and lay down in his place. Now the Lord came and stood there, calling as before, "Samuel! Samuel!" And Samuel said, "Speak, for your servant is listening."

I could start, then, with Samuel, and how I first learned his story late one night when I was nine or ten years old and heard, in the dark of my boyhood bedroom, a voice of my own, a voice so clear and voluble that it stirred me from my near-sleep, and how this voice frightened me enough that I got up and walked down the hall to stand by my parents' bed in the dark, to wake my mother and tell her about the voice, and how she asked me what the voice had said and I told her it had said, "You're going to die," and how, after a soft sympathetic noise, my mother, still lying beside my sleeping father in their bed, told me the story of Samuel, and how I loved that story immediately and yet couldn't help saying, "But what if it wasn't God this time?", and how my mother told me I should pray about it and then I would not be afraid.

So again in the night, as it was for my father in his youth, the child's thoughts led to the parents' bed.

So, as it was for Samuel, the act of discovery is a sleepwalk. The boy rises from bed to walk in the dark, to hear a story, to pray. And isn't prayer itself a sleepwalk? And isn't reading a sleepwalk also, much as writing always is for the writer?

That night I went and lay down in my place, but a story had begun. Already, praying myself back to sleep, I was telling myself the story.

Aren't our roots a kind of sleep whose dream we are?

Essential to Samuel's story is his aloneness before God. Only in the aloneness of his sleep could Samuel hear the voice and know it for the fateful thing it was.

Dear Reader, go slowly, at your leisure.

My Monastic Dwelling at Hood Canal | MARC HUDSON

EACH OF US HAS TOUCHSTONE DAYS and places—when, and where, if we are so lucky, we have lived for a time in a kind of enchantment. One thinks of *Walden*, the radiance of certain passages, and the generally exhilarating tone of the journal that Thoreau kept at his cabin in 1845 and '46. Or of John Muir, twenty years later, following his flock of sheep up into Yosemite Valley, living his luminous days, his first of many summers in the Sierra. A century after that, John Haines, in a quieter key, made his first book of poems, *Winter News*, out of such moments as he homesteaded in Alaska:

> I made my bed in the shadow
> of leaves, and awoke
> in the first snow of autumn,
> filled with silence.

For me that time and place would be the Fall, Winter, and Spring of 1975-1976 on the eastern shore of Hood Canal eight miles north of the village of Tahuya on the Kitsap Peninsula of Washington State.

On a good morning when my head is clear, and I've not drunk too much coffee, I can stand on the deck of the small shore house where I lived that year. More than likely, I am sipping from a mug of green tea well sweetened with a dollop of honey and I am looking down a steep slope of second-growth Doug fir and hemlock at the narrow strip of cobble and drift logs that was the tideland of Hood Canal. Low gray-green waves are leaning forward and tipping over and there are always a couple of sea crows gadding about, and if there is a bald eagle in the scene you can be sure the crows are giving it a hard time. Gulls, plaintive, are a part of that memory's soundscape. Across the mile or two span of water I can make out with my binoculars logging trucks rumbling south on 101. Above that coastal road is the timbered green slope of Dow Mountain mottled with weedy brown clear-cuts. Beyond that working middle distance rise the remote snow peaks of the Olympics, drawing my eyes west and then north toward the horizon where mountain and cloud blur together. Mug in hand, I feel the amplitude of that time and place, and perhaps more keenly now than then, the privilege of that solitude. It was not lost on me. Then I would sit down on the bench built along the north side of the deck, and open, perhaps, my dog-eared Penguin edition of the poems of Wang Wei. Frequently, I would lift my eyes from a poem as if to verify what I was reading in translation.

What was I doing there? A poet of twenty-eight, I had taken a furlough from employment—from my work as an editor for the urban planner, Harold F. Wise, in Washington, D.C. I had saved my money and purchased a year of creative indolence. I was eager to get back to my real work, the making of poems, glad to have found a place more congenial to my imagination than Du Pont Circle. More exactly: I was seeking enchantment (even if I didn't know it). And I planned to catch up a bit on my reading. Lined up on the sill of my picture window were the books of the poets I revered, Walt Whitman, Robinson Jeffers, Theodore Roethke, William Wordsworth, Gary Snyder, as well as a little philosophy—Albert Hofstadter's gathering of Heidegger's late writings, *Poetry, Language, and Thought,* and Hannah Arendt's *The Human Condition.*

I also had in mind a prose project, a series of linked essays which would delve into the nature of dwelling. In a January 1976 entry of my journal, I made a preliminary attempt to define what I meant by that word, which has become in the forty years since, a major trope of ecocriticism:

By dwelling, I mean what I am trying to do here as a caretaker: to listen and watch and let the land come toward me, and meet it somewhere beyond myself; not to intrude but to be here, as a man devoted to knowing where he is. I do this only insofar as I enter into relation with, and encounter as peaceably as I can, the trees, the shorebirds, and the other lives of this shore . . .

These many years later I am still working out my answer. I suppose my relationship with that shore was primarily aesthetic—I spent a lot of ink describing the fabulous cloud archipelagoes over the dusk-reddened Olympics and contemplating what the sun and moon scribbled on the water. Bookish young man that I was, I often saw the Canal through the lens of the poet I happened to be reading. That translucent film is hard to erase even from an old man's vision. But I was in earnest, I wanted to find, still mean to find, how language might become, in Heidegger's terms, an instrument for "the self showing of beings." That Orphic dream, delusion perhaps, has possessed me most of my life—the dream that human language, arguably our oldest tool for mastering nature, can fall under the tutelage of nature and become the means of our reconciliation with our oikos, our ravaged and neglected planetary house.

So I listened: listened to the low waves breaking on the cobble beach below, as I sat reading the German poet Holderlin late into the night. Or on February days when an Arctic high cleared away every residuum of rain cloud, the cold wind pouring from the north, booming in the boughs of the fir trees above my cabin and agitating the Canal so its foaming waters seemed a wild ocean, as I listened even more intently. Which was louder, the surf of fir and hemlock or the actual watery wave lash, was difficult to distinguish.

I listened. On quiet evenings, during ebb tide, I would go down to the cobble beach and sit. I could hear the twitter and whistle of water draining from the shore stones and oyster shells. (I imagined those soft sounds were the breathing and siftings of filter-feeders and nudibranchs.) I would hear, now and again, the ringing wing beats of an unseen scoter and the lap of waves built by a light wind.

I wanted to learn the speech of that shore so I listened.

I peruse my journal in its faded blue ring binder, those yellowing leaves etched by the miniscule letters of my heavy left hand, and wonder, what did that young man learn about dwelling?

Those first days at Hood Canal, I wandered the tideland and marveled at the plenitude of the life there. The Coastal Salish have a saying, "When the tide is out, the table is set." I learned what that meant. I watched the sea crows stalking about at low tide, picking over acorn barnacles and tenantless crab shells with a kind of fastidious ill humor. And I, too, often grabbed my dinner from the tideland, from an oyster bed there. I still bear a scar that I am inordinately fond of: on my right hand, in the notch between my index finger and thumb, a thin white ridge half an inch long, a memento from my oyster-shucking apprenticeship.

Often I came upon the picked bones, the tattered sleeve of scales a bald eagle had left behind. And, sometimes, the fleshy rags of a dead sea gull—a mere wing bone wreathed in stringy veins, its breast feathers soaked with blood. And once, a yearling deer brought down by dogs, I reckoned, its torn belly spilling the slug-like ropes of intestine. The left femur had been gnawed on, leaving the curved haunch bone exposed. Only the lower legs were untouched and showed no signs of decay: they were exquisite, of a soft-cream-colored fur, tapering to hooves sharp and black as obsidian. (A month later I searched for the deer's remains, and all I could find was a spade-shaped bone, possibly its sternum. Around it lay oyster shells heavily crusted with barnacles, resembling teeth on jawbones.)

I seem to have catalogued images of death here, but the tideland taught me that a plenitude of life means a plenitude of death. When I remember walking there, I seem to put down my nose over a hunk of sour bread soaked in iodine, salt, and blood. It is the raw odor of mortality, the stench of things steeped in death. I smell again the tongues of kelp drying in the windrows, the sulfurous oozings of a dead crab. Blood stars someone had placed belly up on shore logs and weighted down with stones. The shore at low tide was a graveyard and a vineyard, the ongoing processes of life and death wheeling about, indivisible.

The common sea star, *Pisaster ochraceus*, with its tough stoic body, came to symbolize the tideland condition for me. It has the fixed sculptural rigor of something lying under the folds of a mortis cloth, and yet moves with the clenched insistence of a powerful hand; a hand, if the embryologists are correct in their inference that the vertebrates are descended from echinoderms, which is groping towards us.

Along with this redoubled sense of the mortality of things, and their enduring life, those early weeks at the Canal put me in touch with words again, and what words lean against. Confronting a huge domed shell coiled like a ram's horn, clouts of veined muscular flesh protruding from its lip, I had no clue what it was, and so had to see it in all its pre-Adamic strangeness. I might have named it "Ram's Horn Snail," had I been Adam. Instead, I consulted Rickett's wise and amiable book, *Between Pacific Tides*, and found its name, *Polinices lewisi*, the moonsnail. A fine name, I thought, full of mystery, night, and gliding silence. Like all good metaphors, it not only altered my perception of the thing named, but the thing alluded to as well: the next evening, I saw the moon with a broad white foot creep slowly up the sky, trailing behind it a faint track of silver.

Nature for me has always been the font of metaphor.

As I muse over the journal I kept forty years ago, I see that I began to learn how to pay better attention, how to listen more carefully. (And I wonder how much of that capacity I learned then that I have lost since in the hurly-burly of my years parenting and teaching.) And I learned how the imagination likes to connect image with image and generate metaphors. And how some metaphors are fecund, and some sterile. These things are but the by-products of my dwelling, gifts of a contemplative year. But had Heidegger not quoted Holderlin and kept at the center of his later philosophy the thought that "Poetically man dwells"? That is, as I tentatively unpack that difficult phrase a little, our dwelling is a making of things, a poiesis, whether of a jug or an axe or a villanelle, that is truly fashioned in light of the realities that brought it into being, as the late Heidegger would have put it, the fourfold—the sky and the earth, the gods and the mortals. Dwelling poetically is the condition of indebtedness. It is the opposite of obliviousness to debt, to the condition of a thing that is part of a "bestand," of reserve stock: the timber on Dow Mountain patiently arrayed for its harvest, to be culled by machines, with no thought of any kind of indebtedness.

So my dwelling at Hood Canal, perhaps, consisted in my poiesis, in my attention to and caring for the ongoing processes around me, and for the words, the shaping of the poem that I was making. Poiesis, then, is not only the actual craft, say, of pottery-making, of throwing clay onto a wheel and fashioning with one's fingers the turning bowl, and then the glazing and the firing of that artifact; it is also the development of the consciousness that can fashion such a vessel. For that poet who would work in relation to a place, poiesis is also the cultivation of attention to the world; it is the making of the mind that makes. Admittedly, my tenure there, of ten months, as it turned out, was too brief to be called dwelling, but perhaps I had lived there long enough to acquire a few intuitions about what such dwelling might entail at Hood Canal.

One of my correspondents that year was John Haines, the Alaskan poet I had met a few years before when he was a visiting professor at the University of Washington, and whom I considered a mentor. In February I had written him a letter, having read a debate between him and John Woods about the nature of poetry that had been published in *The Northwest Review*. Haines had argued of the need for poets to work "toward an insight, say, that makes of experience and perception a particular way of seeing, what we sometimes call the poet's vision." For me, his words were an endorsement of what I had set out to do at Hood Canal, and I wrote him and thanked him for his position. Many years later, John published a collection of essays entitled *Descent*. The title essay was an homage to W.C. Williams's *In the American Grain* and an essay of that same title in that volume. Haines observed that "the main theme of the book is discovery . . . of that true ground underfoot." Williams's insight powerfully influenced the young Haines when he settled in Alaska in 1954. He wrote: "I made the decision—though I could not have articulated it as I do now—to let go, to sink into that country, accept it on its own terms, and make of it what I could."

And yet, to complicate matters, Haines was quick to point out that the exploration of the Alaskan Interior, which had absorbed his daily life, and focused his artistic talents, was not the *telos* of his work. Instead, "it was [his] own interior that [he] set out to explore." Dwelling for Haines was, at least partly, a katabasis, the plummeting of the psyche. But, I would suggest, that his psyche became visible to him through his daily travels on foot, hunting and trapping in the taiga of interior Alaska. Poiesis, and our thinking about dwelling, must reckon with the interpenetration of psyche and nature. Joseph Wood Krutch, in his excellent study of Thoreau, concludes that Thoreau's "retreat to Walden was ... not an escape into the strange, but a digging into the familiar, and, thus, it could become a symbol of that form of adventure for which the only necessary equipment is spiritual."

It is curious that the more deeply Thoreau got to know "that true ground underfoot," the more assured he was that his saunterings had a spiritual inclination. His vocation was walking, and most of his afternoons, between 2:30 and 5:30 p.m., as Alcott writes, were spent in that usually solitary pursuit. If we could trace the almost thirty years of those meanderings on some four-dimensional map of Concord and its environs, I am sure the figure would provide a maze that would beggar the labyrinth of Daedalus, and the creature, the Minotaur therein to be met, might well be the elusive Self, that ultimate Thoreau. So our saunterer wrote in his Conclusion to *Walden* of the ardors of that exploration: "It is easier to sail many thousand miles through storm and cold and cannibals, in a government ship, with 500 men and boys to assist one, than to explore the private sea, the Atlantic and Pacific ocean of one's being alone."

No more than Thoreau was I hermetically sealed in my solitude during my monastic year at Hood Canal. Eight miles down the winding dirt track of the Kitsap County road was the village of Tahuya. I had no wheels that year, so winter mornings, I set out briskly on foot about nine, with my week's laundry in my Kelty pack. By noon I'd be picking up my mail at the post office—there I'd exchange a few words with the friendly postmistress and post a letter or two, then do my laundry and shop at the general store and pack my clean clothes around my groceries, always careful to wrap my bottle of Mateus in a few tee shirts. Then I'd start for home. Occasionally the equally garrulous postman would stop for me and give me a lift a mile or two until the asphalt gave way to dirt. Then while my load of groceries became heavier, I'd make my slow way home, pausing for certain views, at Musqueti Point and then again at Red Bluff. The loops of the hilly road seemed to lengthen through the darkening fir, the alders white and bare in the stream bottoms, as if already lit by moonlight. By afternoon it would be raining. Here and there, freshets were tumbling down through sword fern and salal. Plodding on, the grey landscape made all the more dim by my fogged-up glasses, I'd fall into a waking dream and imagine Basho, a small patient figure toiling at a snail's pace under mountains where the mists resemble grey mosses sprouting from the stones and leaning trees. About the time when the grebe were calling back and forth across the Canal, like crickets on lawns in midsummer twilight, I swung round the last turn and saw, under the dripping black sprays of hemlock, my cabin door.

Later, in the spring, I made acquaintance with a retired couple, Paul and Arden Skoog, lovely people. Once a week, they'd have me for dinner and dessert and a game of pinochle. They, and the kindly employees of the U.S. Post Office, were about the extent of my human community at the Canal. Once a month or two, I'd hitch my way to Bremerton, then take the ferry across to Seattle to stay a few days with friends there.

The visit I most vividly remember was in late May. I came in because Gary Snyder was giving the Roethke Memorial Reading at the University of Washington that year. I was not the only long-haired, bearded fellow in the audience; it seems that most of the counterculture of the Northwest had hitched in from their communes in the Cascade foothills and the Skagit Valley. They crowded the aisles or sat just below the stage. I remember well the impression Snyder made, a small, compact man in jeans, work shirt, and hiking boots. He might have just come in from chopping wood. He had a full rich baritone voice, indeed he even sang, rather finely I thought, his mushroom poem from Turtle Island. And he danced his poems with his hands—beautiful, delicate gestures, a running stream with stones here and there, and sudden pools.

But what most has stayed with me was the story he told of his first residence in Kyoto, Japan in 1956. His first few months there, he said he felt unsettled, out of sorts. The he realized he had not yet visited the Shinto shrines around Kyoto. So he set out on his bicycle one morning and rode to four of them. Each shrine, he discovered, was built beside a stream: they were shrines, he realized, to the deities of the watershed. At each, he clapped his hands, and said, "I am here. I will try to behave myself!" After those introductions, he said he felt a lot better.

Snyder's lifelong project has been to think, and write about, dwelling. He clearly believes it must be ethical. That if the oikos is our house, we need to dwell thoughtfully within it, be hospitable and kind, to take care of our dwelling and behave ourselves. This "watershed ethics," a phrase Snyder uses in *A Place in Space,* a collection of his essays, is everywhere evident in Snyder's work just as we find it worked out in great detail in Aldo Leopold's *A Sand County Almanac.* Willy-nilly, or mindfully, with scrupulous care, we write our signatures on the land of our dwelling.

This ethics is rooted in experiential knowledge. Dwelling, as Greg Garrard puts it, "is not a transient state, rather, it implies the long-term imbrication of humans in a landscape of memory, ancestry, and death, of ritual, life, and work." Any investigation of the ethics of dwelling on the American earth must begin at the least with Thoreau's cabin at Walden, but there are many other way stations in this exploration—Leopold's shack on the Wisconsin River near Baraboo, the cabin John Haines once called home near Richardson, Alaska, Wendell Berry's farm in Port Royal, Kentucky, and, dear reader, the place where you are dwelling these days. We dwell, whether poetically or not.

But the paradigm that most attracts me is Wendell Berry's: dwelling is a marriage between the human and the land, the two not parted even in death. The building of soil is both practical husbandry and precious metaphor. Berry writes in *A Continuous Harmony:*

> A human community, too, must collect leaves and stories, and turn them to account. It must build soil, and build the memory of itself . . . that will be its culture. These two kinds of accumulation, of local soil and local culture, are intimately related.

From that long-term residence on the land may emerge an ethic of responsibility and care. An ethic that must be lived year after year, generation after generation. Culture, like fertile soil, takes a long time, and much thoughtful dwelling, to build.

In 1976, I hadn't yet read Leopold's "Land Ethic"; I knew Wendell Berry only through a few scattered poems. I had not dwelled a long time in one place. I hadn't yet found my mate. I had no children, had not been changed by that deep grace and responsibility, by that joy, and, sometimes, travail. I had not then cared for many years for a brain-injured son, a genius boy locked in his body, nor for a daughter who would become a bilingual special education teacher and a playwright. I did not know the pleasure of nursing a cold beer after tilling a garden, or, a few months later, watching goldfinches with their stout beaks harvesting sunflowers.

I did know with the transcendent certainty of youth that we were one single species in the trembling web of creation, though I was yet but a tourist on this planet. Perhaps that is what the prophet Joel was getting at when he wrote, "Your old men shall dream dreams, your young men shall see visions." Perhaps because their visions have faded, old men develop an ethic in compensation for that loss.

Ethics may be a dour word when compared to "vision," but an essential one for the practice of dwelling.

Yet the young man who had his share of visions living at Hood Canal that bicentennial year of the Republic knew some things that this old man doesn't, except in the faded retrospective of memory. One vision in particular was given to me by that place. It was toward the end of my stay there, in late May, and I had been awake much of the night, knowing I must vacate my cabin before long, and feeling that I had missed a great possibility—"self-involved, lazy, weak, afraid," I berated myself, "I have not done, have not seen all the beauty this place could have given me. . . Truly, I have not fulfilled my promise with this place." Despairing, I fell asleep, and woke soon after dawn.

I opened my eyes. An invisible film lay on the surface of things. Mt. Washington seemed translucent, shot through with light like an iceberg.

Then I saw him. He was perched on a lightning-blasted fir that tilted out over the beach, a bald eagle. I rubbed my eyes. In that aureole light he was brilliant but blurred. His shoulder and wing feathers were storm-dark, black almost, while his head feathers had a saffron cast to them, though not so gold-orange as his beak which shone like a new penny. I thought of the appearance of grasses at dawn, the way their seed-heads are brilliant but their under-leaves, still in shadow, dark as if they were yet rooted to the night. So the eagle, blurred as if I couldn't see the whole of him, seemed a totem of the boundary between night and day, dream and waking.

The eagle peered down and glanced about like a man who is confused and tries to remember where he has put something. But it was a sea-crow, swooping down on the eagle with the regularity of a pendulum, that disturbed him. There is nothing that so mocks the dignity of an important personage as his being nipped at the heels by a Pekinese, so the eagle pestered by the crow lost his aura, dwindled into a mortal bird in a dead fir. But when he tired of this heckling and shrugged those lordly shoulders, and sailed out over the canal, he took away my breath again: from one of his talons hung a large, mailed, glittering salmon.

The eagle seemed to me an apparition of Being, a concentration of presence, as if it had risen from the first waters, made from newer elements than the rest of this faded world.

The morning that ensued was exceedingly clear. I walked along the beach, more alert than usual. Two seals out toward mid-channel were snorting and blowing. A grebe, its breast feathers intensely white, fished, staying under sometimes a full minute and surfacing unpredictably. I ducked back into the woods and started up the slope toward the main road. I saw a large maple in translucent new leaf, standing full in the sun. It, like the bald eagle, seemed like a pure call:

"Turn outward, love things."

"Agape," I remember from a recent homily by our priest at St. John's, means "foolish love," extravagant love that expects nothing in return. That is the love Hood Canal woke in me, that all of us who have spent some time in reverie along a beach, in the mountains or in forests, or hoeing a garden, have experienced. That extension of value to the "biotic community," to all creation—that is the ethos we must dwell in if we are to survive as human beings without diminishing the living systems of this planet beyond repair.

I wonder if solitary communion is the sine qua non for the love that undergirds a land ethic. Or is it, rather, as Leopold believed, fashioned through the collective labor and experience of a living community? And can a poem—or a film or painting—also awaken that love? Side by side those months at the Canal, I contemplated Wordsworth's "Prelude" and the quiet shore at Hood Canal. Some afternoons, I could scarcely distinguish the light beating up from the water from the light borne into my imagination by one of the poem's more luminous passages. That book did seem to me, as Wordsworth hoped it would, "a power like one of nature's."

If I am less sure of that power today, I am more certain that poetry in particular, and embodied language, more generally, is a path toward dwelling. Our dwelling, as Heidegger thought, is in language as well as on the land. Poetry can help bring language into closer alignment with our ancient house.

Yet, antecedent to that, as the pages of my journal confirm, is the revelation of beauty. Hood Canal, that restless span of water, its shield-like gleaming, and the mountains beyond—the Olympics!—bathed in the blueness of dusk. Maybe the lights come from my memory, but they flash and shimmer in those leaves, moons and suns that passed over the vellum of the water, and left their mark on my consciousness. That was the illuminated manuscript I faithfully tried to copy during my monastic year at Hood Canal. In that text, I read my first glimmerings of an ethic of dwelling.

Variations on a Beginning | M. ALLEN CUNNINGHAM

[10]

IN THAT OLD KOAN ABOUT THE TREE that falls in the unpeopled forest and does it make a sound, we have the antecedent for the confused koan of our hyperconnected contemporary moment, which goes: If I am alone, do I exist?

Dear Reader, are you asking this, as you think about your own beginnings—as such thoughts reflect to you the passage of time, your irreversible status as guest in a neverending stream of person and event?

Damn it, we're all so lonely

| PENELOPE SCAMBLY SCHOTT

You can sit across the table
from someone you love, you
just holding your fork.
Or else you're in bed
with your beloved,
hip to hip, your mind racing
through rooms not this room,
decades not this decade.

Maybe you're reading
and you're half asleep dreaming
the ends of sentences no one
has ever written.
Where did you go?

You find yourself
in the chicken coop
of childhood
where the white rooster
with his terrible comb
meets you eye to eye.

Back then you were never
lonely. You thought God
or your mother
or even Santa Claus
really knew
what you were thinking.
You could converse with your first dog.

I am trying to reconstruct the moment
I first understood alone.
Imagine: you approach a break
in the rock face. A passage
opens. You continue chamber
to chamber seeing glimpses of
other people in your life,
but they are walking a different path
through different caverns.

If you're lucky, once in awhile
there's a niche in the rock wall
between caverns
and you can reach your hand through
briefly and touch, sometimes
on an airplane or in the checkout line,
sometimes in bed.

You carry those moments
like keys to a code
you keep trying to decipher.

You write it and write it.
You continue to converse with your dog.

Portable Typewriter on a Small Leaky Boat

| ANNIE LIGHTHART

This is the way I live and maybe you too, if you are compelled
to write about the water and the overhanging trees,
if you keep writing sentences while the shore goes by.
Though no one is reading them, I write even more lines,
and maybe you too, switching the punctuation around
purposefully, like small fish among stones. And maybe
you trail your hand behind the boat sometimes
and then write about it, while the actual hand drips
and finally dries on the keys. Is this an inexplicable life?

The people on the shore live so differently yet have an old
familiar look. They are waving flags, or maybe pages.
We can't know, you and I, because the river moves faster
even as we write it, and besides, we have only one oar.

Echolalia | C. WADE BENTLEY

All day I rehearse in my head
what I will say should someone
speak to me. *I have been ill
but am on the mend.* Then I try it
in British: *I have* bean *a bit peaky*—
but don't think anyone would
buy it. Triple venti extra hot upside-
down macchiato. Nailed it. I look like
someone who would know where
the library is, so I am at the ready:
*keeping the rising sun on your right,
count three paperbark maples* . . . always,
in my head, offering to act as escort
instead. And, of course, something
something about the Tar Heels
(how they are *in with a shout?*), though
soon it will be time to dust off
an aphorism or two about the Cubs.
This could be our year! *Why, yes. Thank you.
I have been ill but am on the mend. I have been ill.*
And perhaps polished enough now
for the cafeteria: *Necessicito*, no, *necesito
mas huevos, por favor.* Yes. *Necesito.*

To the barista at Starbucks who told me Carmel Macchiato isn't the heroine in *Two Gentleman of Verona*

| DOUG STONE

Some coffee orders are short stories,
some are long as *War and Peace*,
great, sweeping narratives of blends,
roasts, flavors, milks, temperatures,
with or without, whip, foam, cream,
shots, double shots, extra shots,
more shots than the *1812 Overture*.
The first time I heard Carmel Macchiato,
Cappuccino, Americano, Frappuccino,
I thought the baristas were talking about
characters in *Two Gentlemen of Verona*.
The complexity of it all hits home when
I'm behind a woman whose coffee order
defines her whole reason for being.
She takes a deep breath and begins her litany
of demands longer than Luther's *95 Theses*,
more complicated than the Treaty of Versailles.
Twenty minutes later when she's finally done.
the great engine of the coffee industry leaps
to life processing her order with hisses,
gurgles, wheezes, whistles, rattles and bangs.
The whole coffee shop seethes like a steel mill.
Then she asks for a pen, takes out her checkbook
and with the flair of John Hancock, she writes.
The woman looks like she expects applause.
But the line that now stretches through the shop
and down the block only glares in stunned silence.
The weary barista nods at me and I move
to the cash register as if to center stage,
clear my throat and recite my little poem:

"Coffee, please.
Nothing more.
Dark and hot.
Let it pour."

Old | C. WADE BENTLEY

The best part is when you first sit on a good bench in a good spot and
the wooden slats have warmed in the sun so they give a bit when you sit
down so that they and everything around you seems to welcome you to the
neighborhood like the brightly colored cyclists who stop to hydrate and
say something about the weather or the smiling little girl tethered to her
mother or the bread truck pulled up to the curb across the street or the bass
beat coming from the open sun roof that shakes the sidewalk beneath your
bones as if all are telling you in this moment that an old man with a hat and
a paperback book is just what that bench in this corner of the city calls for
and so it isn't until you feel the green park growing grey around you and the
solar streetlights flicker on and the dog walkers shorten their leashes and
the chapter you've been reading and had such high hopes for only ends once
again with the aging Icelandic detective holding a drink and staring out
his window that you begin to notice how the curve of your spine no longer
matches that of the bench and how there are fewer people passing by and
fewer still who will look your way and how even those few seem certain you
will turn out to be dangerously rank or drunk or mad or old.

Reflections at the Checkout | LOUISE BARDEN

I keep forgetting I'm a woman
who wears diamonds.
Diamonds, with an S, not just
one well-bred solitaire. Diamonds,
bound into a platinum pool
on my right hand.

I forget the way those stones, that solid weight
Against my knuckle, breaks
reflected light into sparks, cracks
a grocery store's ceiling glow
into such shards a young cashier,
says casually, as I bag
my broccoli, I love
your ring. And every time she does, I stop

for just a moment, trying to remember
what she means and then
what I should say——a plump and wrinkled woman
in jeans and a plaid shirt, a woman
who did not wash
her hair or smear on foundation

before she came to shop. In that split
moment, I calculate
a response appropriate for this girl as young
as I was that day I stood beside a bed
in a dark room stuttering something
polite to the heap of bedclothes, the old
aunt who lay with hands glittering
on the sheets and waited for her nurse
to dole out the next allotted
glass of gin. I stop bagging, just
a second, to hear my own voice years later

on the phone, *Mom, I can't wear*
that. It's a flashlight! But here, now,
in the checkout lane, I catch
myself and answer quick, *Oh, thanks.*
and add, as if an afterthought, *It's a family*
ring, before I go on filling bags
with rice and beans and milk
the way an old woman who wears diamonds should.

Gifts | ELIZABETH KUELBS

Parched quarter mile this track, this lone
runner pounding dust under January sun,
these grouchy bones amusing the empty field –
her mother never made grass laugh. Never. Her

Januarys? Ten-below and why we invented
ski masks. Go get 'em, a stranger yells through
chain-link. I like your stride! Seen, she ekes
speed, catches shade at the curve, jangles into

flow that shushes the grass until joints flag and he
—big man—old tight end? old sprinter?—steps on
the track, stops. Breathe, blow, dangle your arms,
he urges. Swing your hands pocket, chin. Sideways

wastes power. You're at 25%, you'll get 100! He
wants to move her arms so she learns but he stays
in his lane. Thanks! she says, swinging straight, but
in her heart she crosses dust and hugs him like a child.

For Portland teenagers drinking under bridges

| DYLAN D. DEBELIS

Under the 'Made in Oregon' billboard and strung up Christmas lights
the Burnside Bridge bends itself like a crescent moon towards the river.

We are standing in the rain where the waterfront meets the homeless
shelter, pale bodies shivering in their donated sleeping bags
and us in our North Face fleeces drinking gin from the handle.

Under your shirt I move my cold hand against your hot back and the steam
from your mouth forms ghosts that threaten to jump the railing.

There is a barge passing, displacing the syringes in the surf
with an ice breaker and a life boat that has come free. Your singing
pawing at the night like the dew coating the esplanade.

The science museum submarine flicks its spotlights off
and it is too late for our own good. A fog rolls
over the mood ring I bought you for your birthday.
Somewhere upriver the footsteps of a runner and her dog,
while from the church a piano begins to crack its knuckles.

On nights like this I wonder if the city thinks of me,
I wonder if Old Town still creaks with the weight of our footprints on its mud,
if the armory theater seats still retain some of the water damage from our raincoats,
or if the Crystal Ballroom still has a bit of our love lodged deep in its floorboards.

Variations on a Beginning | M. ALLEN CUNNINGHAM

[11]

THE YEAR I STARTED MIDDLE SCHOOL, my mother redid the wallpaper in our house, and behind the old paper in two places—the stairs landing and the master bathroom—she discovered large portraits drawn in charcoal. Both were very finely done, each spookily vivid with personality. For almost a week she left them exposed, and how indelibly I remember the one on the landing, and how I sat on the stairs before it, spellbound. It was the full-body portrait of a man in uniform, a soldier. The portrait was taller than my father, nine feet in length at least, and though the soldier merely stood there, arms at his sides and boots together, and though his face staring out at me was mostly expressionless, his colossal stature alone lent him a vaguely threatening quality.

I couldn't identify the soldier's uniform then, though remembering it today I see that it was plainly German and dated from World War One. He wore a spiked helmet (a Pickelhaube) and side-whiskers, his chin neatly shaved. Adorning the stiff collar at his throat was an iron cross, black straps intersected diagonally across his chest, and his breeches were snugly tucked into knee-high black boots.

For the near-week that my mother left the drawing exposed on our wall, I stared into the figure's smudged charcoal eyes. Why was this soldier there? When, if ever, would he see the light again, after my mother put the new wallpaper up? Once covered over, wouldn't he still be there, always? How could our house be anything but animate after this?

Sure-Footed | MILTON BATES

Carlos was a moralist, which is why
the question made him stop and think:
Are you sure-footed in rough terrain? Fact is,
no one in our squad was surer, walking point.
He had the eyes, ears, and feet of a feral cat,
alert for trip wire fine as spider filament,
disturbed earth, a sniper's safety clicking off.

The rest of him belonged to Western Civ—
Boy Scouts, church on Sunday, the Disney
flick *Pinocchio.* That's what nearly tripped
him up, taking the army aptitude test.
Because he was trying, he told us one day
on patrol, not to show an aptitude
for infantry. *Pounding ground in Vietnam?*
Hell no! Bad enough they drafted my ass.

Still, the question made him look around
the room. All those shaved, anonymous
heads bent over test forms. What if some
computer, blind as fate, took him at his word?
Groped the Braille of graphite dots and sent
another guy instead? It was rough terrain,
but his pencil landed like a cat on *no.*

Carlos grinned, hating the work but loving
the irony. *So here I am,* he said,
same as if I'd told the truth. Then he shrugged.
Don't mean nothing. Desk job can kill you too.

Whose blood is this | DANIEL ARISTI

unraveling over my uniform!? Like in them movies. Impossible to say fer sure, we're all the same liquor inside that we so want to retain—what you see is what keeps the blood from leaving.

Kaboom:

His right hand cut off clean like a flower.

This new guy from Vegas picks it up warm still—feels like holding pizza, he'll say later—and he's yelling up to the drones, *I need fuckin' ice!* Freeze it all, the bullets in midair.

There's a pack of Kools taped to the beige helmet lying on the ground looking like a shit-scared tortoise (Lopez was going for the Latino-in-Vietnam retro look for kicks).

Put in a vase the ice, and the hand in the vase, fingertips to the Sun; open the window. *You'll get it grafted like fuckin' Frankenstein!*

He's thinking so clearly now (in the crossfire he's become alight, an incandescent genius): if he takes out Lopez's severed bough and shakes hands he'll be greeting Death Itself, immense just right behind the cauterized wrist, like all the way to Karbala, so huge that it is crouching down on the sand dunes to fit the uncertain contours

Of a battlefield.

Leave | HEATHER WHITED

You thought you had
prepared to have him home;
for the sling that held
his right arm in place,
for the scar
spread across his shoulder,
down into the dark hair
of his chest that you
will be introduced to later
when he undresses.
You thought you had prepared
to have him clutch you at the door,
his face in your hair,
when you are home and safe.
You had forgotten
that he would not smell the same;
this first embrace,
the smell of army soap,
the feel of the bare back of his neck,
the flinch when he moves his arm.
It is like you hold
a different man
until you breathe,
bury your face
in his uniform
and find the smell of his cigarettes.
You said that you would
not cry in front of him

and so you wait until he has
gone to bed.
At the sink,
a plate in your
in your soapy hands,
tears wet the collar
of your shirt.
A grateful gasp,
the plate
slides from your fingers
but you catch it as it falls
seconds before it hits the floor.
Clutching it to your chest
you say a silent thanks
that there was no noise to wake him.

Two Kinds of Silence | HEATHER WHITED

Footprints on the floor,
half dried,
leading from the
the bathroom back
to the bed.
He has showered and
because he is the army's,
shaved off the stubble
you have memorized
the small differences in
each day
while the week passed.
His uniform,
no longer on
the hanger
where it has
for a week
swirled like ghost
scaring you in the night,
but back on his body,
where it scares you more.
There are still the boots,
you think,
watching him
stand by the bed.
His boots are
still at the door
next to the ones

he wore before,
the older ones,
muddied,
worn down by his feet,
the ones he wore
before he was
England's soldier.
He is not gone
until the boots go on.
He is not gone
until the footprints
have dried.
He sits,
puts his hand on your leg
and you sit up.
He doesn't pretend
not to watch you
walk across the room
or to dress;
later,
you do not pretend to
want breakfast,
to do anything
but clutch the hand
he doesn't use
to hold his cigarette.
Two cups of tea,
half drunk
stop steaming,
his hair has dried
and upstairs

you know that there
will be no footprints
in the shape of his feet
leading back to bed.
The cigarette is finished;
he puts on each boot,
laces them up his
ankles and shins.
You take the car keys
a few minutes later
than you should.
Because the morning
is still a drowsy gray
with a conspiring light fog
you hold hands
as you walk to the car
with the dent in front fender
you made
three months before
on a day he taught you to drive.
The moment before
the engine starts,
he takes your hand again.
You accept in that moment
the silence between two people,
the nods you and he use
instead of words,
that you will soon trade
for the silence of one.

Variations on a Beginning | M. ALLEN CUNNINGHAM

[12]

How BEAUTIFUL A SECRET CAN BE, and what secrets there are in the layers of things.

> If a secret cannot be maintained, we are in a totalitarian space.
> —*Jacques Derrida*

Is the knowing in narrative a surrendering of all secrets? I don't think so, though we're often led to believe this. Let us agree that there are many ways to tell our stories. And yet, isn't every story a form of secrecy?

> All you have to know is whether you're lying, or whether you're trying to tell the truth, you can't afford to make a mistake about that distinction any longer.
> —*John Berger*

Once, in Saint Paul's Cathedral, I heard a voice speaking a prayer that went like this: Lord God, make us humble. Unweave our thoughts, uncomplicate our hearts, that we might lay down our books and step into the dark. Make us empty with longing, that we will seek you.

Some days while sitting and working you merely catch the hem of a thing. And that is a lot. It's a lot.

And in the astonishment that comes, sometimes, of reading, is it not largely a book's having been finished by its writer that astonishes us? That too is a lot. Perhaps it is what matters most of all.

No Telling | JODY LISBERGER

IT ALL SEEMED SO SIMPLE. An ad in the paper. Someone to take him away.

Only Tina isn't ready when the station wagon pulls up by the front walk. She's in the living room by the bay window watering the cyclamen and pinching off the wilted geranium blossoms, wishing the stink didn't stick to her hands. Her husband, Dan and six-year-old daughter, Ruth, are in the front hall, Ruth holding the cat comb, Dan stooping to tie his Nikes, thinking they still have time to groom the cat. Isabel, who's twelve, has already left for the movies with a friend. "You don't want to stay and say good-bye to Snowy?" Tina asked her, wishing Isabel hadn't slammed the door as her answer. Not that Isabel isn't as resigned as all of them about Snowy's spraying. Doors. Baseboards. School backpacks. Shoes lined up at the door. All the vet's suggestions for behavior modification have been useless. Even the valium hasn't been a cure. Unless being drugged into a comatose state can be called a cure.

Tina knows she shouldn't be surprised to see the Crowleys. Albert has called three times—twice to get directions and once to say they might be delayed. "Millie, my daughter, is off at the mall," he said. "Can't be sure when she'll be back. But we'll be along. Maybe around one or two. Maybe."

Maybe, maybe. Tina has repeated these words to herself all morning, knowing that sometimes people call but never show up.

But here's the station wagon, now, rear bumper hanging down like an old gutter, the way-back filled with empty plastic bottles. Tina's terror is almost immediate, though not in the way she expects. Not, what are we doing or how will our children recover, though there's plenty of this, but Snowy's never been in a car like that. How will he cope? For a second she stands there frozen, gripping her watering can, astounded at her own surprise. She cringes as she remembers her gracious words to Albert on the phone when he said they didn't have a cat box to carry Snowy away. "You can take one of ours," she said. "We have lots of empties."

As she walks into the front hall, she nods as she sees Dan take the comb out of Ruth's hand and tuck it under the *Philadelphia Inquirer*, still in its plastic bag on the front hall table. She knows Dan feels the same regret she does. Three months ago, they agreed to give the girls a second cat, a warm, fuzzy, cuddly kitten. The death of Tina's sister wasn't easy on any of them. A soft little kitty seeming like a good antidote. At least for the girls. Show them how life, and love, go on. They never thought that Snowy would start spraying everywhere. When Tina and Dan proposed to the girls that they leave Snowy outside all the time, the girls shook their heads in the gravest way. "Outside? All night? All winter? By himself?"

Tina, Dan, and Ruth stand very still in the front hall as Albert's door swings open and his hand reaches up to grab the rain track to hoist him out. His close-cropped head, long neck, and broad, skinny shoulders rise above the slumping car, so tall and thin all Tina can think of is a card table whose legs once cinched into place take on a whole new meaning. He pauses and squints at the empty sky, presses a hand into the small of his back, and arches slightly before he walks around the front of the car, his legs bony, his khaki shorts seeming sizes too big. At the passenger door, he leans over with such a straight back, like a butler, Tina holds her breath. She watches as a woman, Mrs. Crowley she assumes, squeegees forward on her rump far enough to place her black patent leather shoes on the ground. As Mrs. Crowley emerges, Tina stares in amazement. Not only at the jet black beehive of a hairdo that precedes Mrs. Crowley, but at the way Albert, with the patience of a saint, spreads his fingers over the top of this elaborate twist and holds them there until Mrs. Crowley, relieved of the car, stands up.

How oddly beautiful Mrs. Crowley is. Her tight red shirt and black capri leggings accentuate her short but full figure. When she turns toward the house, Tina can see her perfectly painted red lips, black-outlined eyes, and dark crescent eyebrows. Mrs. Crowley looks so much like a porcelain doll that for a foolish moment Tina wonders if she will walk on her own.

"Shall we go out, now?" Dan asks.

Tina shakes her head. Mr. and Mrs. Crowley, hand-in-hand now, have walked only a few steps away from the car. They are staring at the house—a three-story olive Victorian with a running porch surrounded by scarlet rhododendrons and flower beds. "The house was rotten when we bought it," Tina wants to call out to them. "We rebuilt it ourselves." As she sees the Crowleys scan the flaccid daffodils and denuded tulips, she feels an even greater urge to call out to them to tell them her life has been a bit crazy since her sister died. No time to do the things she's wanted to do. As if her sister's death were any of their business.

"Can't we go out now!" Ruth says, pushing at Tina's back with her tight little fists, squirming and starting toward the door.

Tina is glad Dan stoops down to take Ruth's hand and block her way. "They need a little time," he whispers. "Wait. We need to go out together."

Yes, together, Tina thinks, fully understanding Ruth's beleaguered sigh and scrunched-up face, as if Isabel has given her little sister a key message before leaving. Don't make it easy for them. They might as well be giving us away. Tina wishes she could kneel down and say again to Ruth, "It's terrible, the things that happen in life. Terrible to lose the things you love. I'm so sorry." But she also knows her own words and tears are not what Ruth needs right now. Ruth who has closed the new kitty in her room. The last thing she needs is her mother to come right out and say that at the pound, Snowy's story would be different. "D-E-A-D," she could say. "At least in our version he'll have his own place to be fully alive."

Instead she kneels down at Ruth's level, runs her finger softly along Ruth's lips, and pretends to zip them by way of reminder. Mommy and Daddy will do all the talking today, right? Otherwise, there's no telling what might get said by mistake. Ruth, who often forgets the rules, might otherwise blurt out what Dan and Tina would prefer to keep under cover. Not this death in their family, but Snowy's spraying. Tina and Dan plan to answer all of the Crowleys' questions, but if the Crowleys don't bring up spraying, they've also decided they won't mention it. After all, the vet assured them, "Give him a new place and he'll go back to being his old self."

But the Crowleys aren't coming up the walk. They're facing their car again. Have they suddenly changed their minds? Tina almost starts out the door, but she feels Dan's hand on her shoulder and sees him pointing. Someone else is getting out of the car. A fat girl with long stringy brown hair parted down the middle, covering most of her face. Of course, Tina thinks. How could she have forgotten Millie?

By the time the Crowleys get near the porch, their daughter trailing behind them like a floater that forever hovers in the corner of your eye, Tina and Dan are more than ready to get on with it. Together they push open the door and head down the porch steps. Ruth tucks behind Tina's back, which seems just as well to Tina. To know exactly where Ruth is, watchful but quiet, saving her tears, her explosions, for later. This will all go off as planned, Tina tells herself, Dan extending his hand and giving a boisterous hello—Did they have any problems finding their way?—Albert, his hands pendulous at his sides, grinning and reassuring them, "No, no problems at all." If only Albert's wide grin didn't seem hinged to his whole jaw. If only he didn't tower over them, his white socks stretched so close to his knobby knees that Tina can't stop worrying about where this scarecrow of a man, with a wife and daughter who keep their eyes cast down, will lead not only Snowy, but all of them.

Thank goodness Snowy comes around the corner and gallivants into their circle, as if he will carry them through this ordeal. He leans first against Mrs. Crowley's black pants, pressing like a horse scratching at a rail. Tina watches his white fur come off in layers. Great, she thinks. This will put a quick end to everything. But Albert is chuckling under his breath and squatting down to pet Snowy. And Snowy is rising on his back legs to meet Albert's hand, arching his neck for more scritching, balancing in the air as if he were meant to stand on two legs. And now Albert is chuckling again, louder this time, shaking his head at all that fur, and grinning. To Tina, it's as if one tight string deep in her body suddenly has permission to let go. Maybe she can manage this after all. Can introduce Snowy and make chitchat to assure herself they've read the whole ad—needs a one-cat household—and even remind them, of course she and Dan will take Snowy back if it doesn't work out. She takes a deep breath and starts the whole thing rolling. "I'll bet you can't tell who this—"

The push from behind her makes her instantly stop as Ruth steps forward into the circle, puts her hands on her little hips, and looks up at Albert. "I taught him to stand like that," she announces in a loud voice. "I call it 'Snowy's trick.'" She puffs out her chest as she enunciates each word.

For a split second, nobody says anything. Ruth's entry is certainly not what Tina and Dan have planned, anymore than their desire to remind her publicly that only the adults will talk today. But then again, nor have they planned for Albert's fish grin or his bony knees nearly knocking Ruth over as he stoops down to her level. "Is that so," he says, his voice full of charm. "Well, then, thank you!"

For a moment, it's as if Ruth has become a new person. She beams and nods. But as quickly as the spell came on, it also seems to disappear. Maybe it's the weight of everyone's eyes on her or Albert's standing back up, looming above her, his knees clicking, but she scoots back behind Tina, grabs Tina's shirt with both hands, and pulls the fabric as if to help her disappear. Or maybe she's simply trying to convey to her mother and father—no need to reprimand me. I'll stay back, now. I'll keep quiet. I promise.

Tina smiles nervously. Everyone staring at her now. Or is it through her? Time to fill up this awkward silence, to show them how lovable Snowy is. How lovable they all are.

"I call him the Handsome Sailor," she says, not expecting her voice to boom just like Ruth's. As if they're in competition. But she wants the Crowleys to understand how much they love Snowy, this lord of the neighborhood, who always sits out in the middle of their road greeting all the passersby with his high-arched hello. The same way he greets Tina when she gets home from her job teaching English at the high school. Love me, admire me, he seems to be saying. "Just like Billy Budd," she adds. "Remember that Handsome Sailor?" She waits for the lights of recognition in their eyes. Didn't at least Millie have to read *Billy Budd*? But Millie is as silent as her parents. So silent it's only now that Tina wonders how she could have nicknamed this beloved cat after a sailor who gets hung in the end.

"Tina." Dan's whisper comes like a sylph at her ear. Or maybe he doesn't speak at all. Maybe he only levels his hand very close to his chest, bouncing it ever so slightly. A familiar warning. Turn the volume down, Tina.

She feels the blush rise on her face. She's gotten way off-script. How to get back on? She points to the white hair on Mrs. Crowley's pants, takes a deep breath, and looks right at Mrs. Crowley, willing her to look up and speak. "I hope you don't mind the hair," Tina says softly. Mrs. Crowley looks up immediately, her eyes so firm in their outlines, so encased in the thick dark curl of her lashes, it's as if she'll have to keep her eyes open now forever.

"Oh, honey," she says. "We've had bunches of cats in our time. A whole lot of them. Believe me, they've done a lot worse than this handsome fella." She points at Snowy as she squeezes Albert's hand and smiles. Albert's fish grin comes back. He stoops again to stroke Snowy, not letting go of his wife's hand.

"Sure is a nice cat," he says. "And the little lady is right." He peers up at his wife, his jawbones sticking out like a sharp blade. "We used to have a lotta cats." He keeps scratching Snowy. "Until they up and—"

"Won't you come in," Dan says, pointing toward the door.

If only the Crowleys would sit down in the living room. Dan gestures with a gracious sweep toward the open chairs. Tina sits down in the big arm chair. Dan pulls Ruth onto his lap, letting her legs dangle where Snowy can rub against them. But the Crowleys stand in a clump with the bay window behind them. Tina scans the room. True, it's large and has a bay window. But there are no curtains, linen or otherwise. No famous paintings on the walls or sculptures on pedestals.

"Please," Tina says again, gesturing toward the chairs.

There's a pause so long and quiet you could hear a distant whimper if there were one. In the silence, Tina can't help but feel nervous. What calamity are the Crowleys bringing into this house? How dare they bring another calamity into this house.

It's Mrs. Crowley who looks up first as she presses her very white hand to her breastbone. Tina holds her breath.

"You see—" Mrs. Crowley begins. Tina leans forward a little, not that she really wants to hear, but Mrs. Crowley's voice is soft. "Sometimes, I can't—"

"Can't sit down," Albert says in a little burst. "She hurt her back, you see." He nods little quick nods on his long skinny neck.

"Ah," Tina says, nodding with him, but much more slowly as she leans back. "I'm so sorry," she gushes, her sense of relief coming out stronger than she expects. "I've had back problems myself," she says, wanting them to feel at ease. "Like the time I took Ruth up the rope tow when we went skiing, but wrenched my back as I bent over to gather her in my arms. Or the time I was training for a marathon, running hills and—" But here she stops. The Crowleys' vacant stares are all she needs to feel her face flush. "I know how hard back problems can be," she says quietly. Isn't that the point, really? To show sympathy?

"Oh, honey," Mrs. Crowley says smiling, a little lipstick on her teeth. "I'm afraid skiing and running aren't for me. I hurt myself only on account of my daughter, Millie."

Ah, yes. Millie, Tina thinks, looking right at this daughter who stands behind them, hair falling over her face, shirttails covering her fatness. Now is the chance for Millie's eyes to light up. Please light up, Tina wants to plead. She's almost grateful when Mrs. Crowley corrects her.

"Not this daughter, honey," she says. "This here is Cindy. Millie's at home. I guess I strained my back getting her in and out of her chair." Mrs. Crowley smiles. Albert squeezes her hand.

"Our Millie—you see," Albert says. "She's a quadriplegic. My little lady here must have pulled her back moving Millie's chair. That happens sometimes." He nods that bobbly nod as he puts his free hand around his back and pats a place only Cindy can see.

The silence in the room is like an air bubble pressing so hard in your chest you can't be sure it will ever come out. Nobody moves. Not a limb or a breath. Not even Snowy, who's jumped onto the big bay window sill and is sitting there looking out at the empty street.

"I've been in a wheelchair once." The whisper of Ruth's voice is like a voice from a faraway land. "On a school trip. At the Please Touch Museum," she adds at the last second, then stops abruptly. She looks right at her mother. "I thought it was neat to be in a wheelchair," she adds very softly. "But it must be hard if you have to use it all the time. Snowy will be good for someone like that." She smiles as she leans back into Dan's chest, pulling her lips together.

Albert seems happy to carry on. "Yes, our Millie loves cats. Loves having them in her lap. They calm her real good, they do. Just to touch 'em, you know. They say they can do that to crippled people—old people too. Slows down their heart. We always spoil our cats pretty bad. Give 'em tuna fish and steak—they love it." Albert smiles his fish grin.

"Oh, Snowy loves to eat," Tina can't help but add, maybe because the word "cats" makes her want to ask something else.

"You can say that again," Ruth says kicking her feet against Dan's legs.

For a second Tina is tempted. Sometimes she and Ruth play a "say it again game" for hours and hours, batting it back and forth. But when she sees Dan's eyebrows go up, she knows she needs to push forward.

"You have a lot of cats?" she asks, trying to sound ever so nice.

"Oh, no," Albert says, chuckling. "We used to have a lot of cats until they up and—"

"But do you have cats now?" Tina calls out, seeing Ruth's eyes narrow.

"Oh, no," Albert says, puffing out his chest a little. "We don't have any cats now, which is why when I saw your ad I thought to myself, "Perfect. A boy cat, for a change. Never had any boys before, but I'm aiming to have a bit of company, what with all the little ladies having their own—"

Mrs. Crowley starts to shake her head. But there's no stopping Albert.

"You see, my little lady's health isn't so good these days. The country doctors weren't treating her so good, so's I took her to the hospital near here. They're real good there. Real smart and good." Albert's bony head nods up and down on his skinny neck. "Yeah, I did real good," he says, his grin coming back, ear to ear.

Ruth has become very still. Pause it, she would say. Please pause it.

Which is not the only reason Tina is pushing herself out of her chair, telling them how sorry she is, then stumbling over her own colliding words. "Do you want Snowy? If things don't work out, we'll be happy to take him back." She looks right at Ruth, cuddling deep into Dan's arms.

"You see, the doctors don't give her long to live," Albert is saying. "And the cancer is—" He starts to point at his wife's breasts.

"Do you want Snowy?" Tina says much too loudly, stepping toward Albert at the same time Dan stands up, holding Ruth tight in his arms, both of them knowing this is the moment when Ruth will run up to her room and slam her door, refusing to come out for hours.

Or so Tina thinks, until she sees Ruth stop in the doorway and turn to stare not at Albert, who's saying, "Why, yes. We'd love the fella. Didn't you say you had a box for us?" but at Mrs. Crowley, still patting her chest with her death-white hand.

Tina nearly runs out the door. Maybe she's crazy to grab Ruth's hand and pull her out to the garage, but she can't leave her daughter standing there in horror. As she unlocks the garage and hauls up the door, she tells Ruth to stand right here and wait. The door groans and creaks as the panels curve back on each fold, opening up a gaping crack. Just like the one that caught her sister's finger years ago when Tina closed their garage door and in the midst of her sister's screaming, didn't realize you needed to pull the door up not down to free a finger.

But Tina can't let herself think about her sister right now. Not as the garage door bounces against its top pulleys and she focuses on the ladder up to the second level where they always throw their empty boxes. As she scans the huge pile, she hears herself want to cry out, "Why are we saving all these empty boxes?" But she simply grabs the one they've always used for Snowy—a large Pioneer receiver box with jack-o-lantern triangles cut into its sides. She doesn't throw it down the ladder. She doesn't want to startle Ruth, who's standing there shivering, it seems.

The rest happens so quickly, Tina can barely keep up. On the front porch, where everyone is clustered, Dan gives Snowy to Ruth, who wraps him in her arms, kissing and kissing his head, her tears matting his white fur. Dan opens the flaps of the box. Tina takes Snowy from Ruth, hating the grin she sees on Albert's face, and presses Snowy into the box, where she knows he'll push back, but she pushes down stronger, closes the flaps, and hands the box to Albert, who nods and says thank you and leads his family to the station wagon, where he swings open the back door and sets Snowy in among the bottles. The door groans shut and then he locks it.

As the Crowleys get into their car, Tina tries to pick up Ruth, but Ruth won't let her do more than hold her hand. There's so much Tina wants to say to Ruth right now. How parents love their children no matter what. How sometimes life is cruel. How sometimes you have to do what you don't want to do. But all she can do is grip Ruth's hand as Albert unrolls his window far enough to slide out his bony hand and wave.

But why don't they drive away? Why is Albert suddenly hunched over the wheel? Is he okay? Tina leans forward. Has something happened to him? But he's sitting up now, bringing something to his face.

"Mommy," Ruth calls out. "That man smokes. How can Snowy go to his house?"

Tina hates the words she has to say as she picks up Ruth and holds her close. She'd so much rather run down the walk and race in front of the car so if Albert leaves he would have to mow her down. She could pound on his window and insist he give the cat back. But she knows things like that don't really happen.

"I'm sure he'll be okay," she says through her tears. "I'm sure he'll be okay."

In Good Voice | SARAH BOKICH

There is room in the world for all things,
for the sunrise staining east-facing windows,
for numbers filling the spreadsheets
on every computer,
for dirt kicked up on unpaved roads,
a lonely tin mailbox dented on one side,
for babies growing in teardrop bellies,
and the boy whose nose is flattened against the school bus window.
There is room for missing socks,
slumped and dusty in God's dark corners,
for paper clips,
the ponytail holders you wore on your wrist,
for handfuls of confetti tossed in a parade,
avocado peels curling in as they dry like tiny leather canoes,
for rivers running with sapphire dye,
coastal French towns whose names end in *sur Mer*,
for a hundred black suitcases riding the revolving belt,
for hands that pluck guitar chords badly,
and my childhood singing teacher who stood blond
and barrel-chested with his arms out wide
and said, "I hope you have come in good voice."
There is room for all my days, and yours, dust
trapped between the wood slats of the windows
of your life and pulled taut by a single white string.

Oppressive Bounty | LESLIE MILLS

enough with the
I've had it
can't take any more
I'm up to here with
brought to the brink
can't keep up
drowning

Can't stop reading.
Need to know the news—
local, regional, national, international—
because.
Speed-reading, skimming,
selective reading—inadequate.
I'm overstuffed with words.
From this all-you-can-eat buffet of text
I digest the merest hors d'oeuvres.

My brain is an older model—
needs an update with more RAM.
So, until information can be siphoned
directly into my brain
with a text-feeding tube

Please

NO MORE INFORMATION

Please

The Word Alabaster | GEORGE DREW

> *". . . the slow nudity of November."*
> —Marilyn McCabe

Grudgingly at first, November starts to strip,
a model posing nude for the first time,
timid before all the probing speculative eyes—
a few leaves here, a few leaves there.

And even if the Norway maples around it
have given way to the eternal dictate
of climate, of chlorophyll-fueled depletion,
shedding their leaves in tumults of surrender,

this Norway maple, like the model her
clothing, disrobes slowly, day by day—
only the edges of its leaves stippled rust,
the rest refusing to give up their gold.

Confused, the model shrugs from her blouse,
slips from her shoes, her socks, and trembling,
from her skirt or slacks, her undergarments
like duff bunched around her ankles;

and on the ground a confusion of twigs,
acorns and grasses, and somewhere overhead,
geese by the dozens in unblemished lines
soldiering south until they're soldiering north,

their radar jammed, route confused, November
the way the word alabaster makes you feel:
its glitz of emptiness, for you as for the model,
as of yet implicit, nude not the same as naked.

Variations on a Beginning | M. ALLEN CUNNINGHAM

[13]

DEAR READER, with the steady searching turn of the pages our time goes slow.

Echo Moth | ROBERT VIVIAN

THE ECHO MOTH IS CALLING SOFTLY, softly through the already fading summer days, its wings two petals and powdery folds, echo moth a breath and whisper and caress of a tender breeze so gentle and threadbare it's almost unbearable in its beauty, echo moth saying love is here now and always reverberating down through the ages and every staircase in glissando major, glissando minor and every one of us a secret Chopin bent over the keyboard during a rainy day, echo moth like the torn page of a poem and the gentle opposite of any hard charging, echo moth Doppler and dappler and spiller of bright color just after dawn or during a hot afternoon and the droning of bees abuzz with the music of so much air, echo moth light as sighing and handwritten envelope scrawled to say I miss you, I want you, Quiero, echo moth calling your name, my name, echo moth passing over the open mouth of someone newly dead or just fresh awakened from sleep and distilled from the verb to be, to return, to be happy once more, echo moth a wispy carrier and refractor of trembling leaf light, a small purse of glowing and bookmark of great secret mercy, echo moth directly proportional to all that is good and humble in this world, Monet's grain stacks, an empty soup bowl and sheer panty hose stretched out to dry after much service on a beautiful woman's legs, a mouse carrying a dandelion in her mouth from hovel to hovel, echo moth what we mean when we say Thou movest me, echo moth the ink and urgency of this black felt pen for to write is to gush with dripping feeling and chemical urgency, echo moth in the crust of an apple pie fresh from the oven, in the cries of lovemaking and the sweat of a job well done, the fire wood cut and stacked, the garden weeded and the strawberries aglow with tiny corollas of blossom before they ululate with bursting fruit (and you can hear it going down in bright dimples of redness), echo moth what we mean when we say we are going to church or we are a church ourselves tolling with bells in our mouths the sacred hours, the sacred hours, echo moth the first bird singing before dawn but not the last, no, never, echo moth in every silly love song and the first sentence of a good book speaking softly thereafter, echo moth in the tight loops of a perfect cast, the trembling wormholes of a brook trout caught on a fly so small it's like a dust mote with wings,

echo moth lighter than almost anything on earth, lighter than this piece of
paper or my breath floating up into the sky, weightless and wingless, angelic
for once and without undue striving or grasping or ego-clad presumptions,
oh, this heartbreaking patch of staggering earth and the mighty branches of
an oak tree, my brother, my sister, my one and only not my own manifest of
all creation, echo moth like a wisp of smoke sent to say so much, that it is so
beautiful, uncontainable, incorruptible, a child's whisper, a sprig of blossom,
a light touch on your arm, your cheek, blessing your forehead, today and
always, never ending, leaving its ghost trail in the sacred utterance of every
new name.

Variations on a Beginning | M. ALLEN CUNNINGHAM

[14]

RAINER MARIA RILKE, WHOSE MOTHER, when he was a child, encouraged him in the belief that the remains of a young revolutionary were interred in the parlor wall of the family's Prague apartment—Rilke, in later life, would painstakingly recopy a letter he was writing rather than tolerate the defacing of his gorgeous calligraphy by an ink blemish or compositional mistake.

He wrote some eleven thousand letters this way. It wasn't the idle fussiness of a *raffiné*—it was the work of a poet. "Mon Maître," he wrote to Auguste Rodin on September 11, 1902, "It is not only to do a study that I have come to you,—it was in order to ask you; how must one live? And you have replied: by working. And this I understand well. I see that to work is to live without dying."

Praying in Souzhou | ROSANNA STAFFA

"I'LL BE BACK TOMORROW, DON'T WORRY," Cecilia said to Xiǎo Yú, her goldfish. She placed the fish bowl at the bottom of her small wardrobe and locked it. "If there is an inspection from the Foreign Office and they find you, play dead," she said.

Clothes, money. The simplicity of the preparation for her first trip over the Yangtze River was a bit sad. There was nobody to say goodbye to. The dorm room had a plastic armchair, green linoleum floor, a broken ceiling fan. It had acquired the comfort of the familiar by the end of her third month at the acupuncture hospital in Hangzhou.

Back in May in L.A., she had stood like this in a bare room at the free detox clinic Alpha where she worked as an acupuncturist. Morning, a silvery light. She had arrived early, found the door open. Janet, the counselor, lay curled up against the wall like an animal at the bottom of a cage. Her red hair matted over her shoulders. Rigor mortis had not set in yet.

The following day at Alpha the patients had come to her one by one, wiping tears with their bare hands. They were mostly homeless Vietnam Vets, runaway kids. They had been like family to her. Each one could have been the murderer. She quit.

There was a squalor to the stairs of the dorm, a flutter of insects and a pungent odor of cabbage. No light.

A young man was standing at the bottom of the stairs. Her stepped in front of her in the dark. Her back stiffened.

"*Nǐhǎo*," he said in a whisper.

"*Zěnmeyàng?*" she said.

"The Foreign Office sent me." He was wearing a white shirt, his hair was longish and delicate. His lips had a bruised hue.

"Why?" she said. He looked neat but there was something off about him, like someone who had stayed up all night.

"You want to go to Souzhou?" he said. "I am for guide."

"No need for it." She started walking. He did too. He moved with the fluidity and purpose she had seen in Sword Tai Chi masters. "I don't want a guide, thanks."

An envoy from the Foreign Office could be as dangerous as his appearance was gentle. She had heard of accusations brought against foreigners about casual utterances, *Playboy* magazines and Bibles, and of suitcases that had to be packed fast. No way.

"I'm fine alone."

"A guide is convenient for you," he said.

"No, it is not convenient," she said.

"A guide is very convenient." He turned a delicate face to her but his tone was firm.

"Who informed the Foreign Office that I wanted to go to Souzhou?" she asked.

"*Dui bu qi*, sorry," he said. "I do not know."

"I'm not saying you are some kind of informant, am I? All I'm saying is this is strange. Some things are strange here. Many things. You know what I mean?" She talked too fast, too loud.

"Yes." He looked down.

The road ahead seemed crudely drawn from an ancient storybook. It was hazed by dust, a grey mist that rose and settled at the passage of creaking carts and police sidecars. The buildings were made of bare cement. She had expected a China thick with color. Well, she told herself, this is China. This is the very far you wanted.

"Who are you?"

"Sailor. Today: Souzhou."

"A sailor? No kidding."

"Sailor, yes," he said. "Also, guide."

"You don't work for the Foreign Office, do you?" She wanted him not to. The cadence of his steps was soft. Company felt good after all.

"Not possible. Not education," he said.

"Great, this is wonderful."

"No," he said. "Is very much better job, the Foreign Office." She detected a harsh Cantonese inflection in his voice, or frustration.

"One day you will work for the Foreign Office," she said. His features tightened. Okay, fine, not a chance in hell you will. On the boat she'd buy him a drink, they would share a laugh: foreigners say the darnest things. "What is your name?" she asked. If he would turn up in her memories she wanted to have his name. A name.

"Call me Julian," he said. "You?"

"I am May."

"Easy name."

She had wavered between May and June.

"Why are you in China?" Julian asked. "You come very far, no family." A *gueilo*, a foreign ghost, which is to say: nothing. Why make yourself less than a moth, she knew he was asking. She did not mind being a *gueilo*; nothing was asked of them.

"I am an acupuncturist."

"Acupuncturist, very good."

She willed herself to imagine a moment of leisure; a drink, a little flirting. "Will you have a glass of wine with me?" she asked. Her fake excitement made her a little sad. "Beer?" Say yes.

"On the boat?" he said.

"Well, yes." Have a drink with me. "On the boat."

She fantasized being smitten with him by the second glass. A bit corny, but she'd pretend it wasn't.

"I cannot," he said.

"Why not?"

"I must go to the Chinese section for working."

"I meant after work," she said.

"I must stay in the Chinese section all time."

"Of course, yes." She hadn't thought of the rules. Foreigners here, Chinese there. Okay, fine. She was still glad to have dinner away from the foreigners' canteen, a mosquito-infested bunker with walls painted dollhouse blue. "I know, sure."

"Souzhou. Why?" Julian asked.

"Souzhou is beautiful," she said. She stiffened. It had to be.

"Very beautiful," said Julian, "I have been few times ago."

"Oh good."

"There is a temple in Suzhou," Julian said. "Very famous."

"Buddhist religion?"

"Buddhist superstition," Julian corrected.

She found the party line a bit of an annoying tic. "Superstition," she agreed. It hurt a little. She had often fantasized that the evening Janet was killed, instead of lingering at Alpha, she had decided to go to a Buddhist retreat. Spur of the moment. Nepal.

"You pray at the temple?" Julian said. Their eyes met.

"No, I don't think so. I don't pray. I wouldn't know how."

"Not any problem: I show. I am a good guide for you. If you pray, you must say your name and address first. With so many people in China, it's best," he said.

Janet would have liked to hear of this detail very much.

"Is the temple close to the harbor?" she said.

"A bit close," Julian said. This meant: no.

"Fine. It's okay."

"We have much time for conversation," he said, confirming her suspicion about the distance.

The street was quiet; a few men biked silently, the truck collecting human refuse at night rustled by. A young woman on foot hurried past them. She was dressed in pretty shoes and a *qipao* dress; was probably off to sing in a café nearby. She had a catlike grace.

"Hum . . . I wanted to ask," Cecilia said, "I have not seen any dogs or cats yet. No cats in Hangzhou? No dogs? Really?"

"No," he said.

"In Souzhou?" she asked, teasing.

"They are not any places. Cats and dogs have tax in China," he said. His voice rose, indignant. "Must pay very much. Only rich men can have. For pets, you must be rich."

"For everything you must be rich," she said.

The sparse streetlights flickered on. They walked through the dark patches in between like they were treading water. He kicked pebbles out of the way, lips tight.

"You have a cat in America?" He asked.

"No. No cat."

There were no homeless in China, health care cost a penny, and he was sad about not having a cat. But it moved her. She feared she would stutter, which happened when she was surprised by a strong emotion.

"I have a fish," she burst out cheerily to lighten the mood, then stopped, remembering she wasn't supposed to keep one at the dorm. "At home, in America."

"Of course in America," he said quietly. "Everything and every people of your life is there."

In Hangzhou she had hallucinated patients from Alpha. It gave her a flutter of joy. When she called out they became a rustling of wind, dust. It happened again and again.

"In Chinese we have no word for goodbye," Dr Gan, her supervisor, had said once.

"What do you say, then?" she asked.

"*Zài jiàn,*" he said. "See you again."

The small stand at the corner of Fengqi Lu was still open, casting a pale halo of light on the street. A salesman with thick-framed glasses stood under the fluorescent lamp reading the Hangzhou Ribao, bugs circling over his head. He sold Chinese cigarettes and soft drinks. Cecilia bought two cans, one for Julian. The warm soda left an acid aftertaste.

"Your clinic in America is big?" asked Julian.

"Not big."

"You can pray in Souzhou for different clinic. Better clinic, big."

"I don't want a better clinic," she said. "I don't want a different clinic."

A few men whirred by on their bikes like night birds. We should all stand here and weep, she thought.

"Marco Polo cried when he saw Souzhou," Cecilia said. "He thought of his Venice." She saw in the tightening of his jaw that Julian did not know what Venice was: a woman, a beast, a city.

"Ah good. Veneez, very good," Julian said. Meaning floated between them, out of reach.

"Venice is a city on water," Cecilia said. She sought eye contact, encouraging Julian's understanding by shaking her head yes. "Like Souzhou. It was his home, he missed it."

She thought of Alpha at this hour, the men lined up in front of the door. She knew the sound they made when she unlocked it.

"You have a car in America?" His voice was high-pitched. He clearly wanted her to have a car.

"Of course I have," she said. "In Los Angeles you must have a car." She did not say that her car was eaten by rust and she had let the insurance expire.

At the bus stop to the harbor a malodorous smell lingered, a mix of scat and rotten bok choy. Light came from the unbolted door of a butcher. Bleeding carcasses of pigs were lit by a single lightbulb. Julian and Cecilia stood by workmen in blue Mao uniforms and old women with thinning hair pulled back tight, their skin like crepe paper. No hint of queuing. The men stood up drumming the small of their backs with their fists to stimulate the circulation of qi energy. The women squatted and ate the pulp from cut sugar canes. Julian turned his face to her. She felt he was miserable. She had been good at seeing that, when her patients wanted her to and when they didn't.

"Are you hungry?" she asked him. It was an ordinary question in China. Julian nodded.

"I have sunflower seeds with me." She took a packet of seeds out of her backpack and offered it. He hesitated. "Yes, please. Take it." She looked at the lightbulb above the hanging pigs, the men smoking. If Julian accepted her offer everything would seem less strange. Two people on a trip, sharing a snack.

"*Xie xie.*" He took it.

She watched him eat, spit the husks. He held the bag so she could have some and she did. She felt she was living a special moment, too small to ever share one day. If told, people would think it was simple. From Beijing to Guanjin, nobody ever said goodbye. One could find this simple also.

Julian leaned against the wall of a low building. She did, too. In China an unrelated male and female avoided any physical contact, but their shoulders almost touched.

"Tired?" she asked. The question was considered too personal in China but she was a gueilo after all. A gueilo's tongue knew no sweetness, she was told. One night she had cried at the window watching her reflection in the glass. A clown with big lips, eyes dripping makeup. No sweetness. She had tried to be a better *gueilo* today with Julian, but no luck. She felt for this young man in his good shirt. They both had tried and they weren't good at it. "Are you tired, Julian?"

"I like rest," Julian said. "On the boat, not any rest."

"No?" She watched tiny scraps of paper float like butterflies in a gust of wind. It was a pleasurable, dreamlike suspension of reality. "Always work, work?"

"Not that, no."

"I am a doctor . . . you can tell me anything." I am a doctor.

In her last days in L.A. she had kept the TV on at all times, and finally in the stream of electronic chatter she lost herself. Kill me, men screamed in late night horror movies. Kill me kill me. "What is it, Julian? Long day?" There was a tone in her voice she had not heard in months. She looked at him attentively, and a tiny space cleared in her mind. She remembered how the main part of her job at Alpha, facing despair, had been not so much to speak but to focus.

"I am tired always." Julian shrugged.

"A sleep disorder?" Her voice found a familiar tone. The sequence of intake questions clicked in her head.

"No, no. Sleep is good. The boat give me stomach sickness," he said

"You are seasick? A sailor?"

"No choice. I get the job from government." He was crisp, restrained. "I am a very bad student, I have no choice. In China we take a test, the government look the score and choose you a job. Not changing possibility."

She wanted something to say but went blank.

"It's good that the government takes care of you," she said. The party line on her lips sounded demented.

Julian bent his shoulders as if sobbing, in a shiver of nausea.

"I think sickness: I get sickness," he said. He turned a sweet, gentle face to her.

"There is an acupuncture point you can press for nausea. It's called Nei Guan, Inner Gate," she said, practical. Perhaps too brisk, as he remained silent. He didn't ask where the point Nei Guan was.

"On the boat I am not well. Here I am very strong." He looked birdlike and frail.

She wanted to know how he was living a life without hope. How she could. How people like she and he were tricked into taking one step into it, and then the next.

"Who sent you as my guide?" she said.

The patients used to repeat their lies, over and over, till they became transparent. She knew them all. There was now a suspended moment, like swimming underwater.

"Myself. I hear there are Americans at Zhejiang College. I go to the Foreign Office. If you need a guide today, I say, I speak English, I go to Souzhou."

"Why? Why do you ask?"

"You teach me good English," he said. "You are my teacher. I take the TOEFL, the big test to show you know English to the American government. It is a difficult test. You help me, I do well on the TOEFL, I go to America. You must do very well to have a chance."

Hope is a kind of prayer, Janet used to say.

"I'm sorry, I cannot." She didn't know what else to say. I disappoint. "I don't know how. I can't do it. I can't even do what I love. If I say yes to you it is no anyway. I do not keep my word. In Los Angeles I told my patients to trust me, that I would not leave. I promised I would not do that."

"Difficult promise."

"Yes."

"It is better not to make it."

"I made it."

"You are acupuncturist? For truth?" Julian asked.

"I am."

"Small clinic no money." His eyes retreated from her. "You don't like. Of course you leave."

"No," she said. "I like it. Small clinic, no money. I don't want it bigger, different." A few days before dying, her mother had asked little Cecilia for a holy picture of Saint Sebastian to hold, as if she could trust her pain only to a bleeder.

She looked at Julian, took the wad of RenMinbi bills from her pocket, the Chinese currency for foreigners. He flinched. It was a huge amount for a Chinese. "Use them for a preparatory course for the TOEFL."

She didn't mean to but she seemed to frighten him a little.

"No worries, it's a tip. You are a very good guide," she said. She wanted him to believe her. Now she truly wanted to go to the temple and voice a wish. She could hear Julian's voice guide her through how to pray for the strength to return to Alpha, where she belonged. "We are going to Souzhou. We are going to pray at the temple."

The rattling of the bus startled her: it was coming.

"It is not possible," Julian said. She didn't know if he referred to getting on the bus, taking her money, passing the TOEFL.

"You must do it," she said. "Get on! You are taking me to pray at the temple in Souzhou."

When you meditate you experience a perfect silence, Janet had told Cecilia. She said it filled you with a sense of beauty, a realization that everything and everybody you lost is still yours.

"Julian, I want to go back to my small clinic no money and I want you to take the TOEFL."

The others waiting at the bus stop shifted, crowding in front of the closed door. She heard the metal rasp of the door opening. "Don't be such an ass, I don't care if you don't give a damn, I give a damn. I won't let you give up. Get on!"

A woman elbowed Cecilia out of the way, men wrestled her back. She pushed forward. She made it onto the first step. Julian was standing, dumbstruck. She turned to grab his hand, and pulled him onto the bus. She was shocked at herself. She was touching a Chinese man she was not married to. Fine, watch. Everybody watch. The passengers were shoving their way in, tearing at her grip. She did not let go.

Revival | CHRISTY STEVENS

After your death
I travel to the Himalayan
Country of Bhutan. While high atop
Pele La Pass I pray
that you find happiness
and the root of happiness
—that you are free from
suffering and the root of suffering.
I write your name on a green prayer flag,
Green—the sign of wood,
and string it between the Chim Pine trees
and ask the Wind Horse,
to carry my words to you.

I return to my home in Oregon.
I teach classes
I grade papers
I write reports
I pay my bills
I shop for groceries,
and I eat meals with friends.

My experiences in Bhutan
fade like the setting sun
until one day while hiking,
I stand beside an ancient
Sitka Spruce and
I catch the scent of the Himalayan
air. The Wind Horse draws near
and delivers a message
of prayer flags,
hundreds of red, yellow, white, green, and blue prayer flags
strung across the mountain pass.
I hear the cawing of large-billed crows.

I drink the wind and
I dance the riverstone dance.
I smell the Chim Pines
And I hear the words of my
Bhutanese friend Tshetem Norbu
"I think about dying five times a day," he says to me.

The Himalayan scent dissipates
the Wind Horse departs
and I, surrounded by grace,
am grateful,
knowing that I love and am loved,
grateful for family and friends
grateful to have found a home
grateful for a full pantry
grateful for my health
grateful for my job
grateful for you.

I regret that you had to die
so that I could learn how to live.

Leaving Sicily | CATHERINE ARRA

On the ferry from Palermo to Naples
I am the eyes and blood of my grandparents, an emigrant
clutching a handful of seeds, a small jar of honey.
I want to tell them I know how it was to leave or to stay, how
yearning burns in the breast like a volcano, reversed.

Love eats you, and this is the only way home.

Variations on a Beginning | M. ALLEN CUNNINGHAM

[15]

It is to be noted (Mrs. William James reported) that even after Henry James lapsed into a coma, his hands continued to move across the bedsheet as if he were writing.
—*The Complete Notebooks of Henry James, pg. 582*

IF TO NARRATE IS TO KNOW, then writing is always an act of searching, of seeking out what lies at the bottom of things, the roots and foundations.

To write is to take root.

Turning back to the dark hall, the boy of nine or ten went and lay down in his place.

Dear Reader, the story uncoils and coils again and again.

You've heard this one before. You know it already. Still you say it over once more. Still you listen for the new inflection.

The story is never not beginning.

CONTRIBUTORS

CHRIS ABBATE's short fiction and poetry have appeared in *Common Ground Review, Blue Heron Review,* and *Comstock Review,* among others. Chris resides with his wife in Apex, North Carolina, where he works as a database programmer.

Born in Spain, DANIEL ARISTI studied French Literature at the French Lycée in San Sebastian and now lives in Switzerland with his wife and two children. His work is forthcoming in *Berkeley Poetry Review, Cleaver Magazine,* and *LA Review.*

CATHERINE ARRA is a native of the Hudson Valley in upstate New York who winters on the Space Coast of Florida. Her poetry and prose have been published in various journals online and in print. Her chapbooks are *Slamming & Splitting* and *Loving from the Backbone.*

LOUISE BARDEN has been published in *Sows Ear, Chattahoochee Review* and others, and is the author of *Tea Leaves.* After a career teaching university English classes, copywriting, and magazine writing in Charlotte, North Carolina, grandchildren lured her to Corvallis.

CLARA MAE BARNHART is a PhD candidate in Creative Writing at Binghamton University and recipient of the Samuel Newhouse Foundation Award. Her work is forthcoming in *The Comstock Review* and *Negative Capability Journal.* She lives in Binghamton, New York, with her family.

FREDERICK W. BASSETT is a retired academic whose poems have been widely published. He has four books of poetry, most recently *The Old Stoic Faces the Mirror,* and two novels, *South Wind Rising* and *Honey from a Lion.* He lives with his wife in Greenwood, South Carolina.

MILTON BATES lives in Marquette, MI. He has published several nonfiction books, most recently *The Bark River Chronicles: Stories from a Wisconsin Watershed.* His poems have appeared in various magazines and anthologies. His chapbook *Always on Fire* is forthcoming in 2016.

C. WADE BENTLEY lives, teaches, and writes in Salt Lake City and enjoys wandering the Wasatch Mountains. His poems have appeared or are forthcoming in *Western Humanities Review, Chicago Quarterly Review, Rattle,* and others. A full-length collection of his poems, *What Is Mine,* was published in 2015.

SARAH BOKICH is a poet, freelance writer, and marketing consultant. Her work has recently appeared in *VoiceCatcher* and *Cloudbank.* She lives with her family in Portland.

M. ALLEN CUNNINGHAM is the author of *The Green Age of Asher Witherow, Lost Son, Partisans,* and the nonfiction volume *The Honorable Obscurity Handbook.* His work has appeared in *The Kenyon Review, Tin House, Alaska Quarterly Review,* and others. He is the editor and publisher of Atelier26 Books in Portland.

DYLAN D. DEBELIS is a founding editor of Pelorus Press in New York City. Dylan has poetry published or forthcoming in *Buddhist Poetry Review, [TAR] Literary Review,* and others. His first full-length book of poetry, *Our Graveyard Shift,* is forthcoming this summer.

BRIAN DOYLE is a prolific essayist, author, and editor of *Portland Magazine.* A three-time winner of the Pushcart Prize, he's a self-described ambling shambling Oregon writer. Recent novels include *Martin Marten* and *Chicago.*

GEORGE DREW is the author of five poetry collections, most recently *The View from Jackass Hill,* and a chapbook, *Down*

& Dirty. His sixth collection, *Fancy's Orphan,* is forthcoming. Originally from Mississippi, he lives in upstate New York.

ROBERT HAMBURGER is the author of six books ranging from oral history, personal journalism, biography, and travel memoir, to *Shiraz,* a novel. His three appointments as a Fulbright Lecturer in American Studies have taken him to France, India, and Morocco.

ANDREA HOLLANDER has won two Pushcart Prizes and a National Endowment for the Arts Fellowship. Her book *Landscape with Female Figure: New & Selected Poems* was a finalist for the Oregon Book Award. Andrea teaches at the Attic Institute and Mountain Writers Series in Portland.

MARC HUDSON is recently retired from Wabash College where he taught medieval studies and creative writing. His books of poetry are *Afterlight, Journal for an Injured Son* and *The Disappearing Poet Blues.* His 2007 translation of *Beowulf* was published in the U.K. He lives in Indiana.

ELIZABETH KUELBS writes around mothering three teenagers, running a real estate investment firm, and saving unattended bagels from her Bernese Mountain Dog. Her work has appeared in *Punchnel's, The Hawaii Women's Journal, Vestal Review,* and elsewhere. She lives in Los Angeles.

ANNIE LIGHTHART started writing poetry after walking in an Oregon old-growth forest. Her book *Iron String* was published in 2013. Her poetry has been read by Garrison Keillor on "The Writer's Almanac" and was chosen to be placed in Ireland's Galway University Hospitals. She writes and teaches in Portland.

JODY LISBERGER is a professor at the University of Rhode Island and on the fiction faculty of the low residency MFA in Writing Program at Spalding University. Her stories have been published in *Fugue, Michigan Quarterly Review*, and others. Her collection *Remember Love* was nominated for a National Book Award.

DAVID MELVILLE graduated from The Attic's Atheneum Program in poetry and has read at Portland's Wordstock Festival. He holds an MA from Reed College in liberal studies where he focused on creative writing. He makes his living as an attorney in Portland.

ANN E. MICHAEL is the author of *The Capable Heart, Water-Rites,* and other collections. An educator and Writing Coordinator at DeSales University, she lives in Pennsylvania's Lehigh Valley region on six acres of meadow and woodlot, a place that deeply informs her work.

LESLIE MILLS has been published in *Avocet, Back Street,* and elsewhere. She is a retired music teacher and singer who lives in New York City during the winter and a small fishing village in Nova Scotia in the summer. In both places she attempts to retain or regain her sense of humor.

EMILY RANSDELL's poems have appeared in *The Cortland Review, Tar River Poetry,* and elsewhere. She holds an MFA in Poetry from the University of Montana and coordinates the Manzanita PoetryFest on the Oregon Coast. She divides her time between Manzanita and Camas, Washington.

PENELOPE SCAMBLY SCHOTT received an Oregon Book Award for *A Is for Anne: Mistress Anne Disturbs the Commonwealth.* She lives part-time in Dufur, Oregon, where she writes, climbs "D" Hill, teaches an annual poetry workshop, and watches the wheat grow.

New York resident DAVID SCHULTZ is a certified translator and interpreter of six languages, some of which, along with his travels in their cultures, seem to have worked their way into his writing. He has seen a number of his pieces published online and in print journals.

SOPHFRONIA SCOTT, author of the novel *All I Need to Get By,* loves dark chocolate with almonds. Her work has appeared in *Killens Review of Arts & Letters, Saranac Review, Barnstorm, NewYorkTimes.com* and

O, The Oprah Magazine. She's completed her second novel and an essay collection.

PETER SERCHUK's poems have been widely published in anthologies and journals such as *Denver Quarterly, North American Review, Atlanta Review* and others. His work has also appeared on Garrison Keillor's "The Writer's Almanac." His most recent collection is *All That Remains.*

RICHARD SPILMAN is the author of *In the Night Speaking* and of a chapbook, *Suspension.* His poetry has appeared in many magazines, including *Poetry, The Southern Review, Western Humanities Review* and *New Letters.* He lives in Hurricane, West Virginia.

ROSANNA STAFFA is an Italian-born playwright and author with a PhD in Modern Foreign Languages from Statale University, Milan, Italy. Her stories have appeared in *Story, American Fiction 2016,* and elsewhere. She is a member of The Playwrights' Collective in Minneapolis.

CHRISTY STEVENS is a former UPS truck driver, waitress, and white-water kayaker. She currently teaches at a community college and can be found hiking old growth forests, haunting tide pools, and writing in Corvallis, Oregon.

DOUG STONE is a fourth-generation Oregonian living in Albany. A retired public policy analyst and consultant, his poems have appeared in *Fireweed, Cloudbank, Faultlines,* and elsewhere. His new chapbook, *In the Season of Distress and Clarity,* is forthcoming.

PEPPER TRAIL's poetry has appeared in *Rattle, Spillway, Atlanta Review,* and elsewhere. His recent collection *Cascade-Siskiyou: Poems* was a finalist for the 2016 Oregon Book Award. He lives in Ashland where he works as a biologist for the U.S. Fish and Wildlife Service.

TRAVIS TRUAX graduated from Southeastern Oklahoma State University in 2010. His work has appeared in *Flyover Country, Quarterly West, The Marathon Literary Review,* and others. He has worked at various national parks out west and lives in Bozeman, Montana.

ROBERT VIVIAN teaches at Alma College in Michigan and serves on the faculty of the Vermont College of Fine Arts MFA program. His newest collection of dervish essays is *Mystery My Country.* In 2015, Robert was the first recipient of the Timberline Prize.

HEATHER WHITED graduated from Western Kentucky University in 2006, then worked in Japan and Ireland before coming to the Pacific Northwest. She has been featured in *Lingerpost* and *Straylight* and is a contributor to *The Drunk Odyssey* podcast.

WORDS + PAPER = BOOKS

IT'S JUST THAT SIMPLE

We'll help you take your story from a manuscript to the pages of a book!

Our personalized, one-on-one approach to customer service means you have a knowledgeable human to guide you through the book printing process.

Your books are crafted with pride and attention to detail using high-quality materials, right here in the Pacific Northwest.

Our versatile product offerings, with three different binding styles and a range of custom options, are sure to meet the needs of your unique project. Run sizes from 25-2000 mean a more economical approach than POD, and a nicer book to boot.

Price your project instantly with the speedy quoting tools on our website or give us a call. We can't wait to meet your book!

ACKNOWLEDGMENTS

Hats off to Brian Doyle, Per Henningsgaard, Bill Johnson,
Joan Macbeth, and the folks at Gorham Printing.

Special thanks to Jean Quinn for her Rock Angel donation.

We also wish to thank everyone who is helping make a success of
The Timberline Review. With this issue, we've published over 100 writers
who otherwise might be missing from Oregon bookstores.

We're pretty happy about that.

Community. Craft. Career.

We Are Willamette Writers

Kate Ristau
Author, Essayist, Educator
Willamette Writers Member

Willamette Writers Conference 2016

August 12-14

*Sheraton Portland
Airport Hotel*

Kate Ristau is one type of writer you could meet at the next Willamette Writers Conference. A former writing professor, she currently focuses on writing young adult and middle grade fiction. Plan to join Kate and hundreds of other writers at the largest writing conference in the Pacific Northwest.

Find your community, hone your craft, and advance your career at the Willamette Writers Conference. All writers are welcome.

DONATIONS

Your gifts keep us going.

Each level of donation comes with a mention in a future issue, a one-year subscription, tangible tokens of our appreciation, and our heartfelt thanks.

ROCK ANGEL	$500
PAPER PATRON	$250
SCISSORS BENEFACTOR	$125
LITERATE FRIEND	$75

The Timberline Review is run entirely by volunteers. Your donation will help offset the expenses of printing, distribution, and other associated costs of publication. Please visit **timberlinereview.com** to make your gift, and consult your tax advisor.
Willamette Writers is a non-profit 501 (c)(3) organization and recipient of a Spring 2016 Professional Development Grant from the Regional Arts & Culture Council.

Regional Arts & Culture Council

> "Rarely does a new literary journal begin with such high quality. It's not just that one of my stories was in the premier issue, either. . . . I was, and still am, stunned by the level of professionalism and pure high-end production values *Timberline Review* has achieved. Several issues out, they are only getting better. So, I put this up here for all who want to see their tales find eyes and hearts."

Author Eric Witchey posting on facebook.com/eric.witchey

ABOUT WILLAMETTE WRITERS

Willamette Writers has provided a creative nexus for extablished and aspiring writers since 1965. Workshops and ongoing programs give authors, poets, playwrights and screenwriters of all ages the opportunities to learn and advance the craft of writing.

The Willamette Writers Conference is held every August in Portland. This is where writers meet industry professionals and where careers begin. Registration is open to both members and non-members.

Headquartered in West Linn, Oregon, Willamette Writers is the largest writer membership organization in the Pacific Northwest. Meetings are held monthly in Portland and five regional chapters.

willamettewriters.org

ENGAGE

The Timberline Review keeps the literary dialogue going in the community through readings and discussions and by participating in larger literary events. We'd be thrilled to discover new partners and places to engage with your local library, independent bookstore, or other literary venue. Let us know at editors@timberlinereview.com.

To find out about events coming up with *Timberline Review* authors and editors, check our social media or join our mailing list. Here's our calendar so far:

AUG. 12   PUSHCART-NOMINATED AUTHORS READ AT WILLAMETTE WRITERS CONFERENCE

SEPT. 30–OCT. 2   OREGON POETRY ASSOCIATION CONFERENCE, EUGENE

OCT. 8   SOUTHERN OREGON LITERARY ALLIANCE CONFERENCE (FORMERLY THE SOUTHERN OREGON BOOKFAIR), ASHLAND

NOV. 5   WORDSTOCK, PORTLAND

FEB. 4, 2017   WRITE TO PUBLISH CONFERENCE, PORTLAND STATE UNIVERSITY

The Timberline Review participates in the Community of Literary Magazines and Presses (CLMP) Lit Mag Adoption Program which makes a one-year subscription available to college-level English and literature students at a discount. More info at clmp.org/adoption.

timberlinereview.com

SUBSCRIBE!

1 YEAR (2 ISSUES)
$22 + $4.50 SHIPPING = **$26.50**

2 YEARS (4 ISSUES)
$40 + $9 SHIPPING = **$49**

3 WAYS TO START YOUR PRINT SUBSCRIPTION!

EASY: Mail a check to
The Timberline Review
2108 Buck St., West Linn OR 97068
Make payable to "Willamette Writers, Inc."
with "TR Subscription" on the memo line.
Be sure to include your delivery address
(U.S. ONLY), email address and phone.

EASIER: Call the WW office with
credit card information, (503) 305-6729

EASIEST: Subscribe online at
timberlinereview.com

the Timberline Review

A publication of Willamette Writers

the Timberline Review
SUMMER/FALL 2015

A PUBLICATION OF WILLAMETTE WRITERS

timberlinereview.com
editors@timberlinereview.com
f: timberlinereview
t: @timberlinerev